AS I AM

Written by Alanna Zabel

AZIAM Publishing
www.aziam.com

Dedicated to

That Which Is

TABLE OF CONTENTS

As I Am

If you surrender any and all force, you will align yourself with the realm of truth that is naturally waiting for you. Here you will discover your truest dharma, which is the life that wants to reveal itself through you.

Do you believe you have a pre-destined purpose? Or do you believe that you completely control every event of your life and existence? If you are a believer of the former, are you living the life that you were destined to fulfill or are you struggling to live in alignment with what you believe you are supposed to be? If you believe that you weave every thread of your existence, are you living the life that you created with focused consciousness, or are you living according to patterns and programming set by someone else?

If we look at scientific, cause and effect laws, we are an expression of our thoughts and experiences. Our existence is literally a magnetic, continuously evolving design that moves according to precise mathematical formulas and natural laws, yet the only constant is change. Void of thought, the combination of science and natural, evolutionary process is essentially a go-with-the-flow pattern based on the Law of Attraction. When we step back from any forced or imposed (self and/or other) programming we are best able to witness any previously inputted programs and how they are currently being expressed in our life.

Yet, this can be very difficult, because our societies are founded on control, judgment and selective organization. In order to belong in these societies, we have to act a part that is acceptable. Do the acts we take to belong in our societies resonate with our truest realities, or the realities that we would like to create (depending on which belief system you hold)? If not, how can we unravel untrue programming that is either inhibiting our destiny or blocking our manifestation capacity? Is it possible to return to a state of organic reality while maintaining societal inclusion – living truthfully "As I Am"? Can our finite, linear worlds projecting learned mental illusions harmonize, or even align, with the infinite absolutes and natural truths? I certainly believe so, even though I often feel that I am looking out at a world turned upside-down that believes itself to be right side up. Most of our current day world is a result of manipulated systems perpetually attempting to justify the inorganic beliefs that they are based on.

There is a process-oriented, scientific nature to our existence. Our world is continuously trying to maintain natural homeostasis, despite the imposing, immediate-result plans mankind continues to implement. Being part of this natural process, we all have a specific purpose, or dharma. This is our truest reality. It is also an absolute truth that we have free will to affect our lives however we choose, and impose our will onto our planet and world surroundings. *As I Am* understands these absolute truths, and it understands our infinite personal powers. This book offers a valuable twenty-one day program, called The Dharma Zone, to begin the process of extracting any undesired, externally imposed programming running through our subconscious minds. The program initiates the process of organic self-reflection by distilling extraneous mental chatter and shining awareness on false belief systems ruling one's perspectives. This in itself creates the essential space for one to reveal their true self. To live in alignment with this natural truth is our dharma. To take actions that align with our dharma is living a life of truth. My greatest dream is that one day, the people of our world will unite in complete harmony with the organic, scientific reality that is – where spirituality meets reality and our micro-dharma reflects our macro-dharma.

As I Am details a modern day journey of unraveling one's dharma. It is a flowing expose of spiritual, psychological and worldly lessons combined with day-to-day practices to enhance self-realization. The author, Alanna Zabel, offers concise guidance for the reader to understand the origin of their subconscious programs, as well as how the Law of Attraction kept those programs actively working in their lives. The Dharma Zone is the present-moment space where we are effortlessly revealed. The program includes daily practices of yoga, meditation, physical and mental detoxification and a literal mirror awareness interpretation of one's perceiving reality, called Mirror Theory. Instead of running to a cave to seek enlightenment, this program brings the cave to the reader. *As I Am*'s goal is to integrate this organic way of living into our lives, our dreams and into our world.

As I Am is divided into two parts. Part One offers four chapters which intend to thoroughly describe 1) what dharma is, 2) what traps we fall into that deter us from our dharma, 3) how the Law of Attraction is applied from our subconscious programming and early childhood development – not from our superficial conscious and 4) major personality types that keep us from independent enlightenment, where our dharma and creative power exist. Part Two includes The Dharma Zone twenty-one day program, filled with daily self-reflection, mental and physical detoxification, yoga, meditation, journaling and Mirror Theory revelations.

PART ONE

Chapter 1: Discovering Dharma

"The freedom of the seed is in the attainment of its dharma, its nature and destiny of becoming a tree; it is the non-accomplishment which is its prison. The sacrifice by which a thing attains its fulfillment is not a sacrifice that ends in death; it is the casting-off of chains that wins freedom." ~ *Rabindranath Tagore*

Dharma is an absolute. It can be realized or not; but it is always there, and it is always happening whether we are conscious of it or not. It is not as dependent on our human details (name, occupation, race, opinions, etc.) or our participation, although it would surely be ideal if our worldly life and our dharma complimented each together harmoniously. Again, it is happening with or without us, and a life that is aware of its dharma is a life of deep truth. On the other hand, a life that is unaware of its dharma is often in discord; disconnected, searching and unsure.

The Sanskrit word *yoga* implies *union*. The union of your dharma's natural truth in harmony with your life's choices is the satisfying accomplishment that we hunger for at our deepest level of being. It is the path of least resistance. Yet regardless of this idyllic fulfillment, dharma simply is, and not considering how, it will always seek to find expression to any degree possible. Much like a seed planted underneath a rock searching for a way to grow around its obstacle.

I have always pondered whether my destiny could be altered by my thoughts, actions, lack of actions, behaviors and attitudes. In other words, will destiny happen regardless of me? Will the train return to the station whether I am on it or not? What is my role? If I am an actor on the stage of life, will the play go on without me if I don't participate? Is there an absolute reality always playing on a spiritual "channel" that we can tune in to, listen to and follow or not? Is this broadcast of absolute reality the script of our destiny? Is our human existence a distraction from this absolute reality or an extension of it? Are human choices interfering with global order? And so on.

To answer the questions that I posed thus far, I have hybridized both theories into one. I am a Spiritual Realist. I do believe in dharma. I believe that my destiny is energetic, not as physically specific as a local psychic may color. I also believe that I have the power to express my destiny in infinite forms. Yet, if I do not participate consciously, I risk two possible events to occur: 1) my destiny will not be realized and 2) I risk becoming a victim to someone else's programming.

4

I am saddened by the thought of unrealized potential, and I am greatly amazed to see the perseverance of dharma seeking to be fulfilled regardless of circumstance. It is this power that I surrender to. It is this force that I base my trust and theory on. My motivation for creating The Dharma Zone, the program for realizing one's truest reality, comes from having witnessed enough unrealized divinity in my own life. This sense of loss is best described with the quote by Anis Nin, "And the day came when the pain of remaining tight in the bud was greater than the risk it took to open." I do not want to compromise my dharma for an existence that justifies ignorant fears, false beliefs and manipulated conditioning. I chose to be exactly who I Am, consciously true and powerfully present.

Much of our current-day parenting, unfortunately, has an unconscious tendency to suppress our children's natural instincts just as they begin exploring who they are. We tend to re-direct the child's attention to activities we would like to see them engage in, instead of allowing their organic curiosities to unfold. Subconscious mental programming is actively formulating at this early stage of human life, like an infinitely absorbing sponge. External distractions may detract us from self-realizing and ultimately living in harmony with our dharma. Thankfully, it is never too late to return to that phase of self-investigation and organic self-awareness as a means to begin fully comprehending every fiber of our being, as we are organically, unaffected by external influence. From this unforced, natural environment blooms our personal revelation. When we are in this "Zone", we receive the emotional nectar to begin properly programming ourselves and creating our lives in truthful accordance to our organic truth.

As life is an evolutionary process, it is incredibly helpful to understand the Universal Laws according to which we live. These laws do not change. They are absolute, scientific, mathematical truths. I look at our world, our protocols, our religions, our mean perspectives of reality, and I believe that we are still incredibly primitive as a species. Look at the myths that our ancestors created as their means to understand Nature's cycles and occurrences. To this day we still base many of our cultural rituals and belief systems on these myths even though research has discovered scientific proof negating these old belief systems. Until we understand the reality of Nature's laws, we fall prey to justified human ruling, imposed belief systems, myth, circumstantial realities and semi-truths as a referential means to our existence.

While you go through the process of unraveling any ignorant programs running in your subconscious mind, it is vital to be compassionate with yourself. Give yourself permission to err and to be comfortable alone in the shadow of uncertainty. The search phase of your discovery process is an essential part in finding that which is most true. Try on every shoe until you have a perfect fit. Never lose hope during times when you feel you only have two left feet. This self-compassion is essential in the distillation of "right and wrong" programming within your consciousness. You will simply and powerfully *be,* without any time pressure or shame-filled, process-inhibiting judgments. You will begin to cease the need for approval or permission from anyone else; you will be free to be you, as you are.

During my personal journey, I have experienced ecstatic victories, aggravating frustrations, magnificent miracles, destructive resistance, redundant blunder, boundless awareness, dense ignorance and unexplainable synchronicities. I place no judgment, nor do I hold any trophies. They are all simply part of my process. At the core of us all exist the same desires; we all want to be realized. We all want to connect to what is true. I hope to assist you in understanding what energetic and subconscious obstacles are preventing you from being your truest self. I hope to guide you on the process of removing these obstacles so that you gain access to the Zone where you can create that which your dharma inherently has waiting for you. It is natural for every being to experience abundance, love and light. When we are connected to our truth, we feel good. When we feel good, we do good. When we do not feel good, we do not. If we would like to see a safer, more peaceful world, it starts within each of us.

The formula that I have based the Mirror Theory practice of The Dharma Zone on is essentially a real-time version of world-renowned psychologist Carl

Jung's dream analysis theory. Jung believed that every symbol in one's dream is an aspect of the dreamer's subconscious mind, which he called the subjective approach to dreams. Simply put, each person in your dream is an aspect of you. I apply this theory not only to my dreams, but also to my life. I see that you are me, that I am you, and that, as Thoreau so beautifully said, "It is not what you look at that matters, it is what you see." This perspective will help you to realize the nature of the subconscious mind. It will also empower you to take responsibility for your experiences; removing the self-sabotaging desire to blame what is only an illusion of your own mind. Obtaining this level of self-awareness gives you power to take control of your choices and to make sound decisions since ultimately you are creating everything that you see.

Using the Mirror Theory, we learn to read and understand how the images in our real-time life reflect symbols in our perceiving mind, or psyche. Our mind is translating reality in every moment according to our subconscious mind. Any grooves, or programs, on our subconscious will seek similar experiences and reflections. How the psyche perceives reality depicts how the psyche is conditioned. Once we grasp how our psyches are conditioned, it becomes easier to purify our minds from what is not true; much like working out tension knots in our muscle tissues. When the mind is pure, we are liberated from ignorance and free to "tune" our minds in accordance with reality.

Our dharma is what makes us uniquely who we are. There is nothing to force and there is no one else to try to be; you are already happening. When we approach our life with force or push against what is ultimately a reflection of ourselves, we create resistance. Resistance creates energetic waves or frequencies, which creates karma. When you press your hand into a wall, you can feel the energy pressing back. I am in no way implying that we should not be proactive, creative, dynamic beings. I am, however, suggesting conscious, proactive action in alignment with your dharma. There is no resistance, residue or karma when we act in harmony with truth. It is when we fall out of this direct alignment that we cast a shadow.

Even when we are aware of the natural, unforced choice presented in each moment, we still make decisions, take actions or uncontrollably react otherwise than what would align with this natural truth. This is because our energy fields hold karmas, which are energetic waves resulting from our previous actions, thoughts and conditions. These waves push us according to their force, which can be intensified by internal resistance (what you resist will persist).

Imagine these waves repeatedly hitting the resistance that we impose as a means to keep the uncomfortable subconscious waves from surfacing. The waves multiply and internal storms brew, attracting more and more of exactly what you want to avoid. If one does not understand how to effectively calm these waves, escape mechanisms (food, drugs, sex, etc.) temporarily assist in the avoidance. Temporary highs, fleeting escapes and unconscious state shifts often lead to addictions.

It is possible to reverse these unhealthy states from our consciousness. There is a distillation process to unwinding past karmas. It is based on chemical alchemy, formulaic science and common sense. A screaming child desires to be heard. The cry started from an organic need, but the neglect (or even the illusion of neglect) turned that need into an emotion-laden drama, compiling wave upon wave until the original desire can no longer be recognized. When we become aware of our mental and emotional rhythms, we begin to "tune in" and hear what we need, as if we were attending to that screaming child. In this manner we begin to understand the origins of each wave pattern running through our psyche.

The process of understanding who you are and unraveling your personal unique journey is deeply satisfying. False illusions and inaccurate imposed beliefs need constant feeding and maintenance to keep their façades alive, whereas dharma is dependent on nothing to exist; it simply is. Maintaining illusions depletes our natural life force, diminishes a pure dharmic expression and may contribute to a life of dis-order.

Eventually Dorothy realized that the Wizard of Oz was just a little man behind a curtain, but before he was revealed, she bought into the illusion that led her down the yellow brick road. Her frantic search to find the Wizard who could save her came to an end when she learned that the power to return home was always within her. Dorothy learned that "if I ever go looking for my own heart's desire again, I won't go looking further than my own back yard, because if it isn't there, I never really lost it to begin with." She is reminded that even if she had known this before, it would have done her no good. She had to discover this for herself, and with that Dorothy becomes aware of her own inner power to control her life and returns home to Kansas. Likewise, when our search for an illusionary savior ends we, too, will begin to manifest our innate power to be who we are.

As our minds and bodies become less congested with mental and physical clutter, it becomes easier for our personal dharma to reveal itself. At this point, we will have surrendered our fight to walk the roads of least resistance. As this happens, we will be challenged to value our attachments (possessions, people, memories, dreams, etc.). This will breed a deeper level of appreciation and consciousness for any and all attachments that you do choose to keep – those that facilitate your path and being – as well as the strength to let go of those which hold you back from being you.

Chapter 2: Hypnotic Existence

Everything about our existence is hypnotic and contagious. Each experience we encounter and every relationship we have inputs information through mirrored feedback into our susceptible psyches. The accumulation of this data organizes as programs onto our susceptible minds. Our minds work like computers in that they simply output according to their programming. Yet, we are live, energetic and magnetic beings. Just as computers contract viruses, show signs of stress when overworked and eventually diminish in capacity, our psyches also have threshold capacities that when strained affect our physical and emotional health.

This is the mind-body health phenomenon that our current day and age is now re-realizing. Since our minds are so incredibly susceptible, it is worthwhile to build our immunities to outside influences. This will protect us from the imperfect world -- where other human beings may erroneously imprint inaccurate, self-defeating information into our consciousness as a result of their personal limitations and/or experiences. Everything around us has an influence on who we are. Our media channels choose what news we watch, what trends we will follow and how we are entertained.

Most people do not intentionally or maliciously imprint their limitations onto others; based on their own shortcomings, even parents may fail to provide realistic, objective feedback to their beloved children. In order to break these ignorant cycles, one must obtain truthful self-awareness. When you fully understand who you are, outside perceptions and projections (intentional or not) will have no power to affect you.

"Sticks and stones may break my bones, but words will never hurt me"? Not so true. Our existence is based on the law of *being*. Who you tell yourself you are, as well as what other people tell you, registers as input into your computer brain. Otherwise psychological phenomena such as Stockholm's Syndrome (falling in love with one's captor) and the Milgram Experiment (extreme authority obedience experiment) would not continue to prove true. Hopefully you were never psychologically victimized, as in these extreme examples, but we are all hypnotized to some extent or another.

Over time, you will begin attracting people and experiences based upon the hypnotic blueprint that was established in your consciousness during your early stages of development (and possibly earlier). These programs will continue attracting similar experiences as your life progresses, all the while adding new stimuli and experiences on top of those mental layers until we become Pavlov's newest pet, living a life that we know not how to escape.

What if there was a way to stay organically true to "who you are" while living in a world that is constantly bombarding you with "who you should be"? Can our minds be cleared of undesirable conditioning? Can our mental blueprints resume their organic authenticity? Yes, the mind can absolutely be purified. The process to do so requires patience, persistence and unceasing self-awareness.

Acting vs. Being

One of my greatest passions and talents has been acting. I started performing in local productions in high school, minored in Theatre while majoring in Psychology at college, worked as a Stage Manager at a prominent Buffalo theatre, was the NY representative to Oxford University for a post-graduate Drama school and moved to New York City in my early twenties to pursue my theatrical dreams. Once in NYC, I easily obtained an agent, started with off-off Broadway performances, independent films, commercials, industrials and music videos, all while studying several techniques of acting and performance expression. I resonated strongly with a method of acting called the Meisner Technique. It was so deeply connected with present moment awareness and *being*. And it was not long after practicing this technique that I began to witness shifts in every aspect of my life that I knew were related to this practice.

I was taking a Meisner Technique course in Soho with an instructor named James. Not Jim or Jimmy. James. Like many strong personalities I have come across in my life, James wanted to break me. I laughed too much for his liking. I believe that he defined my laughter as an indication that I was not challenged. Up until this time, I was always fortunate to be cast as the happy, lucky, bright, adorable "girl next door" type, because that was basically who I was – or at least who I thought I was.

James decided to give me an out-of-the-norm assignment, half as a challenge and half purely to ruffle my feathers. Always immersing deeply into my roles, this new, darker character brought me into aspects of being that I was not yet acquainted or comfortable with. Yet, I gave it my all. After rehearsing for several weeks the strong contrast of character clearly manifested as scenarios in my life. Very quickly my life detoured in a different direction than it had been heading.

James gave me the role of a girl who has a major breakup with her boyfriend, moves to Los Angeles, and her life falls apart. I, Alanna, was not dating anyone. I, Alanna, had no desire to live in L.A. (I disdained L.A., actually, as I was a "real" New Yorker). I, Alanna, was completely happy with my life in New York. Yet, within three weeks of intense rehearsals, I watched all of those facts change.

I dove into my role, and I was becoming her. I met with my acting partner twice a week to rehearse. Our classroom was in a high-rise building. One afternoon during my rehearsal, I delivered a wild display of boyfriend disapproval while rehearsing our breakup scene. I actually took my acting partner's belongings (books, sweatshirt, papers, and wallet), flew open the window in our room and threw his things out the 11th-story window to show my disgust and rage at his "character". I screamed obscenities out the window at my "boyfriend." Moments later, I returned to my seat as "Alanna," waiting for instructor comments while my acting partner ran downstairs, desperately hoping to retrieve his belongings.

After about a week of being this new "character," I met a charming, independently wealthy fellow who was getting ready to move to Los Angeles. He developed a serious and persistent crush on me. He asked me to fly to Las Vegas, get married and take a helicopter to L.A., where we would find a home to live. I knew that it was way too fast for me, but there was something very tempting about the notion, and I seriously contemplated it. Because of my conflicting opinions of L.A., I was having an incredibly difficult time conceiving this new possibility. Yet, I did not have enough personal understanding to override what the strong energetic rehearsals had created. I became a victim to my practices of being something and someone that I wasn't, and it carried me away.

I did not have a strong sense of self at that time in my life. Growing up, my mother had very poor communication skills. In order for her to get me to do what she wanted, she heaped emotional guilt onto me when I did not follow her desires. I learned to watch her behaviors to understand what she wanted. Since there was no tangible conversation to track, this silent passive aggressive manipulation seeped into my consciousness, forming a deep, unconscious pattern. Firstly, I grew into a person who never wanted to let people down. The guilt was simply too intense. Secondly, I learned to listen to people's actions instead of their words.

Not being aware of this ignorant conditioning running in my subconscious mind, I justified my "people-pleasing" behaviors as "go with the flow," "seize the moment," "carpe diem" and "you only live once." In no way did my mother intend me any harm, but she may never know the great gift it would have been to teach me to know and honor myself. Instead, she used this means of controlling me to do things that she thought were good for me; because she loved me and wanted to protect me.

Many years later, I ultimately collapsed as a result of this "people pleasing" pattern she established. It occurred when I began dating a man who functioned from the same manipulation – yet his intentions were not pure or benevolent as my mother's. Instead, he had selfish, personal intentions for me and used my developmental programming in his attempts to control me. While healing from the latter experience, I was able to see how my early programming left me vulnerable and disempowered. Our personal relationships magnetize from our early subconscious programs.

Was it a coincidence that one week after the idea of moving to L.A. crept into my consciousness that my bi-coastal agent landed me an audition in L.A.? At the time it seemed to me that Destiny was pulling me to L.A. Or was it the repetitive practice of my newfound character's experience of *being* the "girl who moves to L.A." that was attracting the means to fulfill the accumulated mental input? Or are they one and the same? Needless to say, I moved to L.A. on a whim and a prayer, had a breakup and my life fell apart. I was in a new city, and a superficial city at that. I did not like it at all, as I had thought. Yet, I had metaphorically checked in to *Hotel California.*

After a few auditions in L.A., I was eager to retire as an actor. The audition waiting rooms were filled with "actors" who lacked training and oozed insecurity, peroxide and fillers. It was nothing short of insulting to a classically trained performer. Of much greater importance, though, it led me to the realization that I no longer wanted to play somebody else. I was convinced that I ended up there as a result of my acting class assignment back in Soho, and I was done playing other characters. I no longer wanted to be directed by other people according to what they wanted me to do. I wanted to understand who I was and to do the best job playing *me*.

If we are not actively programming ourselves according to who we truly are, we are vulnerable to being hypnotized by others. And though we are in a New Age world where many experts are explaining the power of "being," "mantra," "Law of Attraction," and so on, I simply do not trust anyone else to hypnotize me as accurately as I can. No one else can possibly know who I am as well as I do. Only I can strengthen my sense of self. Only I can connect with my inner truth and knowing. Only I can eradicate delusion from my consciousness. Only I can click my magic slippers. Consistent self-hypnosis in alignment with natural truth will lead to self-realization.

Chapter 3: The Real Secret

Being a yoga instructor, and part of new age communities, I hear people referring to The Law of Attraction on a daily basis (as described in the book and DVD *The Secret*). Yet what I find missing in this documentary is crucial for any true manifestation of desire. The Law of Attraction will always run according to the *subconscious* programming of the mind, not simply what one has taped on their Vision Boards. The mantras and vision boards are surface level actions, and if the subconscious is not addressed and purified, one is simply placing the cart in front of the horse, so to speak. The superficial conscious cannot magnetize nearly as strongly as the subconscious mind can, and the subconscious will always cancel out the conscious if there is a conflict in belief – it has stronger roots and deeper reactions. If there is no conflict, and the conscious desires reflect the subconscious mind, the vision board will quickly manifest into reality. Deep transformation of subconscious beliefs misaligned with our desires will only result from the conscious non-reactive distillation of these the beliefs and/or attachments.

We were all born without having any problems whatsoever asking for what we wanted. As infants, we kick, cry and scream for our desires without fear or shame because we want to be fed when we are hungry. The ego aspect of our psyche develops as a self-protective mechanism very early in our lives. It serves as a means to ensure survival. If during our early childhood, our needs continued to be satiated consistently and appropriately, our ego develops by forming healthy relationships with our caregivers. This healthy ego will continue evolving into higher levels of communication -- much like a dog learning to sit, speak, roll over and lie down in exchange for the food and love it desires.

If, however, our needs are not met, our ego develops in response to survival fears. Since the ego is formed directly from its reality, it assesses what will be necessary to get what it needs. Using the same example, a dog would seek any opportunity to secure some source of food. An example of the affected human ego development is a sociopath. This severe personality disorder is programmed to manipulate others for his/her own gain. At the deepest level of their psyche, their actions are triggered from an affected means for survival.

Once the ego is formed, it either learns to comply with community and societal rules as a progression of its healthy relationship skills, or it learns to rely solely on itself to fulfill its needs, feeling isolated and abandoned to provide for itself – regardless of societal rule. A healthy ego has a realistic sense of self and is able to consciously fulfill its needs within the community it is part of. Since an affected ego has not developed relational skills, it becomes anti-social and separated from community.

The definition of this affected ego is the general new age reference to the word "ego" – dark, manipulative, secretive, negative, selfish, etc. Protective mechanisms often develop as means to defend these less attractive shortcomings in communication and near-sighted self-survival. This affected aspect of ego will learn to lie, cheat and steal as a means to survive, since the healthy, conscious means of fulfilling one's desires through communication and community were never developed.

Pure Soul

Our dharma begins as pure, unforced soul potential waiting its time to be realized. There are four major forces at work affecting our individual and collective dharma. The first factor is our universal, collective subconscious soul. Imagine, if you will, that there is a collective energy soup, so to speak, where all souls source. At first, before we are conceived into physical existence, our only psychological input is from this collective unconscious. The universe is an entity in itself, constantly organizing and purifying itself according to natural, scientific laws. Metals find magnets, thoughts find energy and energy finds form. Our souls came into human existence out of this process, and this is where our dharma organically originates. Your soul knows what you are manifesting to be, and there is a reason and purpose that you manifested specifically as you. You are part of the universal evolution process.

Somatic Input

As early as conception we are subjected to stimuli from our environment that reflect, harmonize or distort our source soul frequencies. Sounds, visions, colors, sensations, tastes, smells and so on. Before our conscious minds have developed, we cannot yet process these new experiences into any kind of order, nor do we have reference experiences to categorize them. Instead, we absorb them through our feeling body. These new somatic sensations that result from the interactions with our environment register as imprints onto our subconscious mind. This is the second factor affecting our dharma. The subconscious mind is very much like a recording album; it is impressionable. Our experiences and reactions to our experiences set grooves that will continue to play on all levels of consciousness, whether or not they harmonize with our soul's purpose.

These grooves resonate frequency signals that attract similar experiences and reactions. This is the very reason that we continue to see repeating patterns in our lives. While we continue to unconsciously repeat the same patterns, we continue to deepen these grooves, intensifying the subconscious attachments to the source experience.

Karma

With time, we build a database of reference points from our experiences. We begin perceiving, evaluating and forming a conscious mind. Once this is developed, the third factor comes into play; that being our personal karma, which is based on the law of cause and effect. This is the re-action of our thoughts, beliefs and actions in response to our subconscious feelings. Our responses and reactions form our karmas. Karma is simply a Sanskrit word that implies action. A ball thrown against a wall will propel back equal and opposite to how the ball was thrown.

Similar to the word, ego, our societies have erroneously placed incorrect connotations onto the word, karma. It is not a bad omen or a curse. Karma is simply a direct response from our thoughts and actions. Our emotional consciousness will self-impose our own punishments and/or rewards according to what we already have defined as good or bad, therefore it is a limiting belief that a particular action (ex: stealing a loaf of bread from a market) will create bad karma. In this example, the person stealing the bread may believe that a sick child will be cured from the nourishment. Therefore, the thief believes his actions to be good, negating any assumed negative return of energy. One day that thief may see the market owner crying from her business losses. At that moment, the thief may realize the extended effects of his actions; at that time, he may self-impose negative punishment from his newfound awareness.

Based on what is imprinted on our subconscious minds (the grooves), we generate actions, re-actions and beliefs. For example, if we enjoyed the taste of milk, we will want more. The sensation from drinking milk created a pleasurable memory onto our subconscious mind. This memory triggers an action to seek more. Since we are completely dependent on our caregivers during our early development stages, we begin the dialogue to get more milk. Since we do not yet speak or understand a common language, we cry from the pain of not having the pleasurable milk. This cry is often responded to with exactly what we sought – the warm, soothing milk. One of our first grooves has been imprinted onto our subconscious and the addictive cycle of our bi-polar world has begun.

Each action of seeking more milk creates a deeper groove onto the subconscious mind (according to how intense the hunger is) where the initial somatic sensation was imprinted. As the pleasurable sensations develop, the pleasure principle also links the painful sensations of not having the object of desire to the same experience.

Contrary to the pleasure principle (but equal in energetic charge) is a reactive negative response. Negative reactions also deepen the grooves of source somatic sensations, but the pain is in the repeat experience, not in the absence of. If we did not like the sensation of milk as an infant, we cried when it was present and calmed when it was not. It is clear to see how a bi-polar, co-dependent, addictive personality can result from an extreme of either experience; pleasure seeking or reactive avoidance. We are ultimately shaped and programmed from a collection of our likes and our dislikes.

In this book, I am only focusing on present-life karmas. If we do recycle and experience many lifetimes, then we probably attract similar karmas at re-birth to continue learning where we left off the last time, in hopes of fully transforming them the next time around (and if those lessons still need to be organized in the collective soul). I am only focusing on the accumulation of present-life sensations, thoughts and actions.

You can see how these three factors begin to consolidate a person's core belief system, whether or not these beliefs are accurate or realistic. Imagine a clear and calm ocean with only water. There are no sea animals, no sea vegetation, no waves or activity. This is your pure subconscious mind. When you add fish, sea animals, weather patterns, wave currents and so on, external stimuli begin affecting the ocean. The ocean reacts in response to these stimuli, resulting in the formation of waves and currents. The ocean will naturally return back to a calm equilibrium when void of stimuli, as it continually seeks homeostasis. The waves are karmic by nature. From this example, one can see how storms develop in our minds, and how reactive behaviors result in situations far from what is organic.

Conscience

Out of this formulaic process develops the fourth factor affecting one's dharmic expression. That is one's conscience. Our communities typically reflect back rules and regulations, merits and demerits, all of which regulate behavior. One's personal conviction and conscious motivation to regard ethical or moral principles ultimately mold their conscience. During the period when the ego was developing relational skills, it was also learning awareness of others. If the ego continued to properly develop, the seed of a conscience was planted. If relational skills were not learned, the conscience was not conceived and the anti-social personality continues developing it's own beliefs, rules and regulations that serve only themselves.

Soul vs. Shadow

The soul is a constant; separate from the human expressions of I am _____ or You are _____. The soul simply is. I am. You are. Nothing attached to it, nothing affecting it. The soul is the part of you that is broadcasted from the collective unconscious that you are localizing in your physical form. Our souls can be experienced through meditation, quiet self-reflection and intimate, present moments. The soul is Feminine by nature, as it is void of force. It is process oriented, compassionate, source-centered and infinite. The ego is our human self-protective mechanism. It is Masculine by nature. It is goal oriented, quick to judge, defend and survive. It calculates and it is finite.

The soul and ego dynamic can be expressed as a human partnership. Have you ever been amazed watching a couple working seamlessly together, communicating and respecting each other to create a mutually desired outcome? Have you ever been horrified watching a couple bickering, blaming and fighting for control over every step of a project?

How do you work with others? How are your relationship skills? How do you want your internal marriage of soul and ego to function? A healthy inner relationship occurs when the ego acts to support, reasonably protect and truthfully express the soul. A dysfunctional inner relationship occurs if the ego became affected in early development, where it became a slave to its shadow (the accumulation of ignorant beliefs and fears). The enslaved, affected ego abandons the soul's expression of dharma to feed its deep subconscious hungers and reactions. This forms an even thicker fog of illusion between the ego and the real self.

In Jungian psychology, the shadow is described as the part of the unconscious mind consisting of repressed weaknesses, shortcomings, and quite interestingly, as well as instincts (discussed later). The shadow-serving ego will seek to project its insecurities (somatic grooves): turning a personal inferiority into a perceived deficiency in someone else. It is the shadow (not the ego) that is defined by the dark, secretive and negative energy. The ego is merely the drive to maintain survival and an affected ego has been misguided to serve the shadow instead of the soul.

The source insecurity still hungers for a taste of milk, but the accumulated shadow does not know how to consciously attain it. Guilt, shame and lack of confidence merge into the hunger, ultimately affecting everything related to the pleasure principle: love, sex, joy, giving/receiving, food, material abundance, etc. One can only suppress these needs for so long. When an opportunity to feed appears, the affected ego goes about feeding in a covert, selfish manner (stealing, raping, overindulging), followed by some form of purging (if there is a conscience).

I have witnessed highly functioning individuals with dark shadows that are barely recognizable on the surface. They have controlled their life in that their shadow is not easily seen. They have created a predictable comfort zone, typically padding themselves with the security of financial wealth and the service of others to keep their fears or hungers from surfacing. Yet even the smallest amount of loss will strum the deep groove of pain and loss that is still unprocessed in their subconscious mind. This individual has enabled himself; he is not liberated, for his deeper mental state is still vibrating fear, hunger and anxiety – even though the polished surface state appears in control, satiated and content. An underlying state of dis-ease is difficult to suppress forever; it will eventually surface.

In order to enlighten the shadow, these two entities -- soul and ego -- need to align and cooperate with each other. They must form a marriage from the most difficult relationship dynamic possible -- the relationship of the unconscious meeting the conscious. Yet, the affected ego has been programmed to feed and protect the shadow. If the shadow is exposed, the ego's false purpose will be threatened as becoming nonexistent – unless it realizes its true purpose.

As I mentioned earlier, the ego has taken the brunt of extreme negativity as the scapegoat of new age jargon. I want to change the daunting illusion of the ego as being evil. Our creation myths and religious stories tend to illustrate good versus evil. For us to truly accept reality, we must see that this is not a universal law. True, we have negative and positive, darkness and light, but "good" and "bad" are emotional judgments we humans have attached to these realities in means of controlling majorities. Our universe would not have sustained as long as it has if we were divided in motive in this way. Our human ignorance of this universal law could very well be contributing to a fundamental breakdown of world unity here on our planet.

The universal law is based on attraction and creation. Absolute reality supersedes negativity and division. Light extinguishes the dark. There is no force that wants to hinder you from your truth and power. There is, however, a force that constantly wants to guide you *to* your truth and power. When you realize that you are supported in your efforts for truth and positive power, it should naturally feel easier to participate in the process of self-realization.

Jung also believed that "in spite of its function as a reservoir for human darkness -- or perhaps because of this -- the shadow is the seat of creativity." This creativity sources from heightened awareness for survival. Cultivating awareness increases personal power and creativity. Have you ever noticed how some of the most affected egotistical people are also some of the most creative, magnetic and successful? We have a choice on whether we use our egos to calculate means of deception and illusion, or to consciously nurture our innate capabilities for greatness. The former modus operandi takes a lot of energy to maintain. It generally results in exhaustion and humiliation. The latter M.O. is eternally rewarding and effortless.

The unconscious energies and uncontrolled reactions in our shadows need to be organized in our psyche. The more unorganized energy that accumulates, the more confusion and chaos that permeates one's energy fields, seeking recognition and release. These karmas, genetic memories, somatic vibrations and collective unconscious broadcastings all need to be recognized if we seek complete self-realization and enlightenment. Yet, becoming fully conscious of these highly charged frequencies and karmas may likely disrupt our current beliefs as they shed light on the temporary illusions that we have built our lives upon. It is not an easy process, but it is completely possible. When it comes to healing these subconscious grooves, less is always more.

If one believes that holding a green pillow will provide complete protection while traveling on an airplane, this person will likely feel a sense of security in this belief while boarding a cross-country flight. If this person becomes aware of the possibility that the green pillow lacks such power, then their entire safety may feel thwarted and jeopardized. This truth revealing, organizational process of reality can be painful and confronting, but it does not have to be burdensome. There is work involved in unraveling the true you, and this work will be eternally rewarding.

After completing The Dharma Zone program, you will feel lighter and more connected to your source. As you embark on living a cleaner, less congested, positively charged lifestyle, you will inevitably begin to not only cleanse yourself, but also those around you. You will notice people shifting consciousness as well as their behaviors in your presence. The Sanskrit word for "teacher" translates precisely as "supreme example." When we lecture, judge, condemn, ridicule, demand and so on, we are not nearly as powerful of a teacher as simply "being" that which we want to illustrate. This does not dismiss the power of verbal instruction (especially conscious and respectful communication) but always remember that your consciousness and presence will be the ultimate force in making a difference in the lives of those around you. Your energy exudes your wisdom. If you are living in your truth, it will communicate through your actions and being.

As the consciousness of the planet rises, you will notice an increased number of people resonating and communicating with this higher truth. We will shift towards a loving, patient, compassionate, organic, process-oriented Feminine paradigm. This is what will heal our planet, if this is to happen. I hope that it does. The higher consciousness seeks relationship awareness. It desires the less conscious to become more aware, for that is when they will recognize their reactive, destructive patterns and actions. Once the realizations of these negative actions are understood, positive change is likely to follow.

Hunger

The hungrier that you become, the greater will be your desire. The greater your desire, the greater will be acquired. The greater your acquisitions, the greater will be your loss. And the greater your loss, the greater your enlightenment potential. During my years of leading fasting yoga retreats, I witnessed how difficult it is for most of us to be hungry. As I mentioned earlier, we may have camouflaged our shadow's hunger for security, love and affection with state-altering pacifiers such as food, sex, material possessions, status, and so on. Through the fasting and detoxification process, our true emotional hungers inevitably surface while food is temporarily restricted. Once we recognize what the crying baby within us really wants, we have the opportunity to provide for our deeper needs and to heal ourselves.

As a young girl, I was raised with a passionate, religious and devoted mother who taught me about the prophecies of Nostradamus, the Virgin Mary apparitions, the power of prayer and the prophesized dangers that would occur globally if the people of our world did not change their ways. When I was eight years old my father was laid off from work. The financial stress was apparent to my brother and me. As a means of being a smaller burden to my parents, I began eating less. I prayed and dreamed of a way to provide for my family. The stress took a toll on my parents and they began to argue more often. I sought out ways to soothe them and to help them to be kinder to each other. I often went to the top level of my childhood home, hung my head out the window and screamed for the world to "PLEASE WAKE UP!" -- because my personal survival depended on it.

Many years later, during intense years practicing yoga and meditation, I dissolved down to my deepest and truest desires. I once again found this little girl as a major part of my ego, a girl minimizing her foods and praying for peace. Coincidence? Hardly. It was fortuitous for me that there happened to be popularity in being a yoga instructor, relationship psychologist and health nut by the time I realized I had developed into one, but I needed to get beyond those subconscious reactions that formed in response to my parent's situation if I wanted to find the true me. – behind the sweet-faced yoga teacher.

Much like the comedian who wanted to make his unhappy father laugh, or the musician who wanted to impress her critical mother, when the desired goal is unattainable, the skill level of the one seeking to reach the desired goal may increase phenomenally, and even receive world acclaim for their developed talent. But oftentimes at the core of the acclaimed artist is a child who does not feel successful, since the original objective remains unchanged -- in this example; the unhappy or critical parent was not impressed or changed. This is how we end up with masters of their trade like Jim Carrey, Michael Jackson, Madonna, Oprah, and so on.

Why We Are Here

Most early childhood years are perfect for dharma realization in that they serve also as a padded incubation period in which the child, powerful in his seeming powerlessness and dependence, is simply a pristine mirror to what is. If we can trust that we attracted our parents and families prior to birth as part of the universal organization process, it is easier to comprehend that the obstacles in which we are to overcome are imprinted onto our subconscious minds before we know any better; maybe they match the specific manifestation of the collective unconscious that we personally came into physical form to process. These grooves will set a tone and magnetic frequency for the child's life, and will continue unconsciously forming the adult life if left unprocessed. We are more easily influenced when we are in this phase of our lives. Maybe if we knew any better, our collective unconscious dharma and karmas would not have a chance to imprint.

The ancient Hebrew discipline and esoteric teachings of Judaism, called the Kabbalah, explain the relationship between an eternal creator and a finite mortal universe. The essence of Kabbalah teachings can be illustrated in a metaphoric example. Clean water remaining clean water is pure, but it does not hold transformative power in its naturally pure state.

An alchemic power is central to Kabbalah. In this manner, pure water that became dirty, then transformed back into pure water accesses the infinite power of transformation. Our Kabbalistic, transformative power lies in our abilities to purify that which is not true. Re-programming our subconscious minds is the most powerful action we can take.

According to the law of Kabbalah, it is in the moment of this transformation that we make contact with the 99 percent realm of Light, or divine, eternal power. By resisting our reactive impulses (and hungers) we create consciousness. Reactive behavior creates electricity in the moment they happen, but as previously illustrated, they ultimately leave darkness and addiction in its wake.

Celebrities are fascinating to watch. They typically make grander attempts to unravel their deep-rooted issues, and in their process, we get to witness what guru they turn to, which pills they pop and what dramas they create; not to mention what addictions they cling to, and how they overcome the obstacles in the way of their star-light. They usually have an incredible drive to overcome their obstacles, and this is typically why they become stars.

Madonna is a fabulously clear example of a person who appears to have deep-rooted abandonment issues. Madonna's mother died when she was very young – when she was five years old. Interesting that even her name is an obvious nuance for her life's challenge. Madonna's ravenous hunger for stardom, power and attention could be relative to the hunger she felt for her mother's love. Like most youth, she was probably unable to understand this heavy emotional void at her young age. As a means of survival, her ego developed to protect her wounded feelings of loss and her vulnerable desire to be loved. Did she, like many, attempt to substitute her subconscious hunger for her mother's affection for the love and adoration of others?

In my theory, no one could sufficiently replace the source of what she was looking for. Not many can replace pure motherly love. The media has illustrated a woman carnivorous in dating. Could this be why Madonna appeared to tire quickly with any futile attempts of others? Not even the adulation of the entire planet praising her could fill the void of missing her mother, and that may very well be the force behind her stardom. Along the way, she became the icon of Goddess -- strong, powerful, beautiful, independent, seductive. What was missing? True peace, at least it seemed. Until a time came when it appeared Madonna grew content; when she became a mother herself. Becoming a mother may have allowed her to tap into the source of what she was starving for and to transform her obstacle into light. This is Kabbalah. This is transformation.

For several years in my early thirties, I lived a very yoga-esque, go-with-the-flow life. During this time I encountered incredible experiences of unbelievable synchronicity and opportunity. I was so positive and happy that I laughed in my sleep. Whatever I needed instantly manifested. I felt like the luckiest girl on the planet. I lived on honey and fruits. I had bathing rituals for detoxification and I practiced yoga and meditation at least once a day. I was clean, healthy, positive, fit and openhearted. I was an advocate for world peace, and I was a good person. I was in The Dharma Zone – but I did not know it at the time.

Like an unavoidable ocean current, my lifestyle led me straight to my core programming. I spent years practicing non-reactivity, detachment of desire, dissolving physical restrictions and surrendering to every moment. The practices led me right to a remote, untainted mirror of Self. And there, just one layer surrounding my dharma was my ego, like a gargoyle protected the tabernacle of my shadow. Face to face with my shadow, the abyss of my deep-rooted unconscious fears and ignorance that was inhibiting me from my divine Self -- who I truly am.

Wanting to understand my ego's relationship with my shadow and to fully rid myself of ignorance, I had to face the parts of my subconscious that continued to generate feelings of being neglected, denied, rejected, betrayed, hungry and unheard. They say that the dark night of the soul precedes enlightenment, but I had no idea the extent of internal warfare that I was about to engage in. Since every aspect of our consciousness, realized and unrealized, is continuously seeking to align with our divine plan or dharma, my yoga and meditation practices eventually led me to face the shadow I had been unaware of.

Each of our experiences reflects each of our mental states of being, much like a movie projection sources from rapidly moving still film images being passed through light. What we see is an illusion or image in front of us; it is the movie on the screen, mirroring our mental state of mind, sourcing from our mental movie projector. Two people looking at the same ocean may see two different images according to their different mental programs. One may see the miraculous healing waters of our planet, and the other may see a murky pool of sharks. What you see is what you sought to find. In the realm of absolute truth, void of personal perceptions or labels, it is simply an ocean; it simply is. When we begin to perceive our world from that same realm of absolute truth, we will step into present-moment reality. It is there that we exist, as we are.

How can you extract preconceived notions and pre-judged perspectives from your mind so that you are able to experience your divine soul, living in absolute reality, as it is? How can you start to see others as pure soul, recognizing soul meeting soul (the word, "Namaste") instead of seeing others as a projection of your subconscious grooves? Think of how a child would perceive that same ocean. The child is not bringing past experiences or imposed influences into their perspective. They are seeing it in its truth.

There are countless similarities in all of our world religions. Many believe in an Almighty God or Goddess. The personification of a God- or Goddess-like energy is one of omniscience and omnipotence. We are told that this Divine energy knows everything and sees everything and yet still loves unconditionally and silently. As we embark on our own journey towards this divine, or super-human state, we can learn to apply these same, God-like qualities to ourselves. Can you know everything (the good, the bad, and the ugly) and still be non-reactive and compassionate? This is the pathway to enlightenment, and it starts within.

Chapter 4: How Personalities Disorder

As parents and partners it is crucial to understand the responsibility of our relationships. The law of karma (cause and effect) governs every aspect of our existence. Whatever enters our consciousness has an effect. Every word you speak and every action you take is registered on those around you, and they will be affected somehow. There is a causal reason for every aspect of a person's personality. Our accumulated experiences greatly influence our personalities, our relationships and every aspect of our health and being.

Children are impressionable and dependent. It is imperative for parents, teachers and guardians to understand the responsibility of having such power and influence over a child's life. There is a similar responsibility among adult relationships, but later relationships typically stem from development relationships. Therefore, later relationships may very well be secondary situations that one attracted according to the relationships from their upbringing. Regardless, we should all tread lightly with the hearts, minds and bodies of others. It is wise to develop such consciousness that one will never take action to diminish the life force of another being, be that through thought, word or action.

When our personality is forming during our developmental years, the absolute most important element for establishing a healthy personality is secure attachment to our caretaker (most often this is one or both of our parents). A child needs to be consistently cared for during this utterly vulnerable time of absolute dependency and uncertainty. When we are consistently cared for, communication begins and trustworthy relationships are established. When a child learns to trust that his needs will be met, the essential foundation of security is established. A strong sense of security is a major building block for physical, mental and emotional health.

A child will develop a greater capacity for all forms of security throughout his/her life (financial, emotional, physical) as a result of having known security during early developmental stages. This does not guarantee financial wealth, for example, but the capacity is there. On the other hand, a child who did not develop security at an early age may not feel comfortable with financial wealth later in his life. He may obtain wealth, but bring with it a perpetuating fear of losing it, as he had only known a similar lack.

These examples show how abundance consciousness affects out abilities to receive wealth, but this consciousness is not isolated to financial abundance.

There is enough abundance for all beings to have a rich life of love, light and wealth. When you are steeped in feeling abundant and free, there is nothing you find lacking in yourself. Yet, if you feel that you are lacking abundance in your subconscious mind (insecurity), your actions will stem from lack. These actions will source from desperation and fear; thereby they will attract more lack. Abundance consciousness can be developed at any stage of life, but it is especially beneficial to instill this in our children.

Another important element in any relationship, including all family relationships is non-judgment. Judgment suppresses the natural learning cycle of being human. If we feel afraid to tell the truth because of imposed judgment from a parent or partner, we suppress the truth, which goes right into the shadow's closet where it will ferment, multiply in intensity and begin to etch a deeper groove of discord onto our subconscious mind.

My perspective of this non-personal approach to personality analysis is intended to educate the reader to the causal effects of what they are objectively witnessing. In this manner, I hope to avoid any unnecessary or inaccurate judgments placed upon individuals who are in a state of mental misalignment with a personality disorder. I believe this approach will not only provide information on how to individually unravel personality dysfunction, but also to widen the gap of compassion in our communities. There is always a causal reason behind every occurrence.

Following this approach, the therapist, friend, counsel, parent or partner becomes a mirror to their client, friend, co-worker, child or partner. They have enough self-control that they will not risk imposing deeper wounds onto the wounded by projecting any subjective advice and personal motives onto the person they are working with. Nor are they imprinting any inaccurate perceptions based on their own past experiences. They are mindful not to abandon, neglect, judge, direct or ridicule in any way. This is the arena of healing that we all deserve.

A lot of treatment/analysis modalities today begin by labeling an individual with a disorder. This definitive assessment gives the power to the disorder. It is important to acknowledge each person as divine, and to understand the circumstances that contributed to the development of their disorder. This allows the road to healing to become self-empowering; it allows one to *return* to wholeness, instead of believing they are ill, wrong or bad.

Functioning Dysfunctions

The more aware of personality disorders that you become, the more you see varying levels (even very low grade or dormant) of these misaligned patterns in those around you. Here is a list of classifications for common traits and types of people stemming from personality disorders. I have casually

46

labeled them by their dominant characteristic. Included are examples of how these personalities can develop in our early childhood development years.

1) <u>Sugar</u>

The Sugar personality type loves and often needs to feel sweet. The taste of sweet comes in many forms from the obvious cane sugar and fruits to alcohol, and even in the form of many recreational drugs like heroine. Those who justify excessive use of honey, agave or natural sugar supplements aren't fooling us either. They are simply wiggling away from the cupcake stereotype to a healthy alternative to feed their need for sweet. Essentially, it is the substance induced "happy high" that the Sugar personality desires. It is always telling to observe the base state of a person seeking out a substance to control their emotional state. What are they uncomfortable with in that base state that drove them to seek a change beyond their personal control?

The Sugar personality's body type can often appear "puffy", or swollen from the inflammation that excessive sweets cause in the body, even though they may exercise often (and they most likely do). This type of personality disordered is often borderline, bi-polar and/or co-dependent. They hunger to be loved so badly; in order to attract the bees, they provide the sweetness.

When the sugar wears off and they are not feeling the surge of "love" from their sugar-induced high, they grow unhappy, and they seek out more.

This exasperates the addiction cycle. Sugar people are rarely in a state of balance. The need to keep their veins filled with sweetness is typically their coping mechanism to avoid dropping into reality. On the surface, they appear to be very generous, but as with any imbalance, underneath the surface they are often the opposite; insecure and needy. They never learned relationship skills to progress beyond the "I am cute, therefore I get attention and love" phase. As a result they learned to manipulate others as their means to win more love.

Borderline personality disorder (BPD) is a condition characterized by impulsive actions, rapidly shifting moods, and chaotic relationships. The individual usually goes from one emotional crisis to another. Very stressful or chaotic childhoods are commonly reported (e.g., physical and sexual abuse, neglect, hostile conflict, and early parental loss or separation). Mood disorders, substance-related disorders, eating disorders (usually bulimia), posttraumatic stress disorder, attention-deficit/hyperactivity disorder, and other personality disorders frequently co-occur with BPD. Although emotional instability and impulsivity are very common in adolescents, most adolescents grow out of this behavior. Unfortunately, if relationship skills and self-awareness are not developed and utilized, this emotional instability and impulsivity persists and intensifies into adulthood.

Now, as you can imagine, there are varying levels of this personality. There is a fellow yoga instructor that I know in Los Angeles who is the poster girl for Sugar. She offers wine at all of her yoga classes, she is hyper gushy ("I love you! even though I don't know you because you have something that I want"). Her behaviors are especially obvious when she sees an opportunity for gain or personal attention. She is addicted to Facebook and social networking – feeding off of communication and positive comments from people, and appears devastated when there are none. She is obviously not creating any overt harm to others (only to her dharma), and being a low threat to others, this kind of dysfunction is often enabled, rewarded and unrecognized, especially as it falls into the guise of "new age positive". Hyper should not be mistaken for positive.

Clearly, the more toxic that the physical substance is, the more residual effects there are on the brain and body. Speed, crack and heroine have a much stronger and more toxic effect on the brain and body than wine and honey, but essentially, they feed the same subconscious grooves and over-stimulate similar areas in the brain. Since non-reactivity liberates us from subconscious grooves and karmas, the greater the state change is, the more difficult it becomes to not react, making this cycle innocuously addicting.

Justified: A non-profit employee

Affected: Alcoholic, drug addict, diabetic

2) <u>Fire</u>

The Fire personality type is intense, and their intensity drives them to move. Their movements create friction and that friction exudes magnetic warmth and desirability. These individuals are sought after by others, but fleeting in being caught. They are brilliant at creating stories and illusions as a means of distractions, and they dread being caught in their lies. Essentially, they, too, are hungry. The Fire personality's hunger is far more intense than the insecure, emotional Sugar personality type. They hunger to be recognized as "God's gift". They are typically very passionate, logical yet oftentimes angry and reactive.

The Fire personality type can be selectively avoidant, since they believe that they are always right. If someone or something does not agree when them, they will pay it no mind. The diagnostic personality disorder most associated with the Fire personality is the narcissistic personality disorder (NPD). Narcissistic personality disorder is a condition in which there is an inflated sense of self-importance and an extreme preoccupation with one's self. A person with NPD reacts strongly to criticism -- oftentimes with rage, and unwarranted defensiveness. They take advantage of other people to achieve their goals. They tend to have feelings of self-importance, and they exaggerate their achievements and talents. They are preoccupied with fantasies of success, power, beauty, intelligence, and/or perfect love. They require constant attention and admiration. They disregard the feelings of others, lack empathy, have obsessive self-interest, and pursue mainly selfish goals.

The grooves of hunger began to etch onto the subconscious mind at a much later developmental stage than the Sugar personality. Fire personalities most likely received a lot of love and attention during their early development. However they were not prepared for the rest of the world not being up to speed by not treating them with the same idealization and care. A child who was privileged will grow into an adult who expects the same pattern to continue. The poster heading of a narcissist is the development of a superiority complex. If they were not socially prepared with realism, they have a difficult time being just another "Joe". This is actually a normal, healthy phase in adolescence, but if proper relationship skills and self-awareness are not cultivated, the immature patterns and beliefs perpetuate into adulthood.

Fire personalities like control. They have great need for stimulation and they prefer living on the edge. Physical addictions are common with the Fire personality as well – addictions to sex, coffee, cigarettes, spicy food, fitness, and image.

Justified: An attorney or a celebrity

Affected: A bank robber or rapist

3) <u>Stuffer</u>

The Stuffer personality type is often the person who seems to carry the weight of the world on their shoulders; yet, for whatever reason, they do not communicate, process or demonstrate their feelings. As a result, this personality stuffs down their emotions with food, sedative drugs (pain killers, marijuana), suppressive avoidance (tension) and/or becoming the victim of controlling relationships. Growing numb to how they feel, they tend to have a difficult time understanding their emotions, which typically results in a difficult time expressing their feelings.

Stuffers also have a difficult time being emotionally vulnerable with other people. They are more fearful of hurting other people's feelings and/or being shamed if they do attempt to express themselves. As a result, they conform to others, listen to others, care for others, but struggle taking care of themselves. Stuffers stuff for a variety of reasons, but it is very unlikely to be related to physical nourishment or deprivation. A stuffer often stuffs to suppress the feelings they are uncomfortable with: sadness, shame, fear, loneliness or emotional distress.

Stuffers use the above-mentioned substances to induce a false state of comfort, to deal with emotional and physical pain, reduce anxiety from social pressures, to suppress personal desire, to avoid the feeling of loss (misidentified as hunger), or to avoid guilt ("eat what you're given"). Not everyone learned to

52

be in tune with his or her natural hunger cues. Parents want their children to eat what is provided, not realizing the emotional shame and guilt they are linking to food. This subtle emotional connection leads future Stuffers to uncontrollable, irrational emotional eating and self-sabotage. Succumbing to guilt eating denies and ultimately weakens one's personal power of self-control.

The result of such early conditioning is that 1) this person no longer knows how much to eat and when to stop and 2) everyday emotions trigger eating. Stuffers are full of self-doubt. Making decisions becomes stressful since they never learned to trust their own instincts, desires and logic. Instead, they've learned to please others at their own expense, and since they don't trust themselves, they grow dependent on outside approval to make decisions. The Stuffer may eventually become depressive due to their poor self-control and limitations in self-expression.

The correlated personality type associated with a Stuffer is the dependent personality disorder. Dependent personality disorder is a chronic condition in which people depend too much on others as their means to meet their needs (emotional and physical). Dependent personalities feel powerless and a need to be taken care of develops, along with a fear of being abandoned or separated from important individuals in his or her life. Symptoms include: 1) difficulty making decisions 2) lack of responsibility 3) difficulty expressing disagreements with others 4) difficulty initiating projects 5) taking extreme measures to avoid displeasing someone or losing their support 6) feeling uncomfortable alone 7) urgently seeking relationships 8) unrealistically pre-occupied with fears of being left alone to care for themselves.

Justified: An assistant for an aggressive, domineering and high-powered executive

Affected: A victim of domestic violence

4) <u>Airy</u>

The Airy personality is completely removed from reality. They do not want to know, and/or cannot handle, reality. They tend to lack down-to-earth common sense. These woo-woo fairies want to place their personal destiny into the hands of street corner psychics. They want to literally believe in, attach to and defer to blue-faced gods and myths of old and new (instead of realistically identifying with the symbolism of what they represent). They tend to be religious, superstitious, spiritual, dependent and possibly delusional. There are similarities to the Stuffer, except that their means of coping differ. The Airy seeks an illusionary escape from worldly realities, whereas a Stuffer numbs him/herself as means to avoid them.

Airy personality types gravitate towards new age communities and cults. They want to believe that there is a definitive, external reason for their life and that someone else has created it and controls it. You may know the type – the

54

gypsy-like yogini driving a VW bus to full moon ceremony? Since food is a grounding factor to one's emotions, the Airy may likely avoid food. This behavior can be easily justified as perpetual purification fasting. They easily fool themselves into believing their enigmatic ways are based on a true, unseen reality; this only feeds the external delusion and avoidance of the present-moment reality in front of them.

A delusion is a belief that is provably obvious to be false. The belief in this untruth indicates an abnormality in the affected person's content of thought. The key feature of a delusion is the degree to which the person is convinced that the belief is true. A person with a delusion will hold firmly to the belief regardless of evidence to the contrary. Delusions can be difficult to distinguish from overvalued ideas, which are essentially unreasonable ideas that a person holds, but the affected person has at least some level of doubt as to its truthfulness. A person with a delusion is absolutely convinced that the delusion is literal and real.

Delusions are categorized as bizarre or non-bizarre and as either mood-congruent or mood-incongruent. A bizarre delusion is a delusion that is very strange and completely implausible for that person's culture; an example of a bizarre delusion would be that aliens have removed the affected person's femur bone. A non-bizarre delusion is one whose content is definitely mistaken, but is at least possible; an example may be that the affected person mistakenly believes that he or she is under constant FBI surveillance.

A mood-congruent delusion is any delusion whose content is consistent with either a depressive or manic state; for example, a depressed person may believe that the world is ending, or a person in a manic state believes that he or she has special talents or abilities (that they, in fact, do not), or is a famous person. A mood-incongruent delusion is any delusion whose content is not consistent with either a depressed or manic state or is mood-neutral. An example is a person who believes that thoughts are being inserted into his or her mind from some outside force, person, or group of people, and these thoughts are not recognized as the person's own thoughts.

Delusions of control and thought broadcasting are usually considered bizarre delusions. Most somatic, grandiose, persecutory and religious delusions, as well as most delusions of jealousy, delusions of mind reading, and delusions of guilt would be considered non-bizarre. Airy personality types are often able to socialize and function normally, apart from the subject of their delusion, and generally do not behave in an obviously odd or bizarre manner. This is unlike people with other psychotic disorders, who also might have delusions as a symptom of their disorder.

Beginning in early adulthood, the Airy personality may have developed a pervasive distrust and suspiciousness of others and their motives, leading them to make-believe friends and fantasies. One or both of their parents may have been unfaithful and/or divorced at an early age with reasons not understandable to the child, again leaving them to create their own explanations. They may also have been raised in very religious or superstitious households, where uncertainties were law and they were to be believed without question. In their uncertainty of reason, Airy personalities make up reasons to believe in the unseen, mystical magic or they fall prey to extreme cult beliefs or leaders as a means to explain what they do not know.

Justified: A yoga instructor or a priest

Affected: A paranoid conspiracy theorist

5) <u>Avoider</u>

The Avoider personality type can be very frustrating in relationships – work and/or personal. They have traits similar to the Stuffer, mixed with Fire and Airy characteristics. In short, they are not comfortable outside superficial relationships where they can control how they are perceived and what expectations are placed upon them. The Avoider does not become involved with others unless they know 1) they are held in high esteem due to their fear of rejection and 2) that no one needs anything from them due to their fear of responsibility. If an issue comes up in a relationship that threatens their esteem or lack of responsibility, they will fly away, making conversation and/or resolution very difficult. They can be physically and emotionally unavailable, and like the Airy type, they often seek to escape reality.

The Avoider has similarities to the Avoidant Personality Disorder, although they may not be completely anti-social, even though they may be prone to anxiety. They may feel inadequate in intimate relationships, afraid of not being accepted socially and afraid of responsibility for fear of failing the task at hand. This personality type skates away in efforts to keep from interacting with people when they know (or feel) something is expected of them. The Avoider seeks to avoid 1) being disliked by others 2) intimate relationships 3) perceived conflict and 4) responsibility.

Similar to the Stuffer, the Avoider attempts to ignore what they are feeling. They may sometimes use substances -- alcohol and/or drugs -- as their means of escaping reality. The Avoider seeks a buzz or a high, whereas the Stuffer uses food, which grounds and/or depresses the feelings instead. The Avoider does not always use a substance as a means to avoid; they often use direct avoidance or a manic state as inappropriate responses to reality. By simply flying away, sticking their head in the sand or laughing off the situation as unimportant until the perceived threat has passed, the Avoider deflects intimacy, accountability, their emotions and fears.

Justified: A comedian

Affected: A homeless person

6) <u>Wall</u>

Have you ever met a person whom upon meeting them you feel an immediate jolt of resistance? After making an introduction and an attempted impression, you find that nothing you exhibited was accurately perceived? The Wall personality projects their perceptions before a person is able to display who they are or what their true intentions were. The Wall tends to be very judgmental and pre-occupied with their mental perceptions; so much that they cannot perceive each moment organically. Wall types state their views and observations in authoritative terms; they decree what is right and wrong, what should and should not be, what is good or bad. This person is rigid and fixed. They often have very standoffish personalities, making them harder to get along with, which may interfere with their lives and the lives of those around them.

The Wall types can be associated with Obsessive Compulsive Disorder. OCD is characterized by a rigid adherence to rules and regulations, sometimes to the detriment of the individual or the people around him or her. People with this disorder typically follow rules to a fault and are generally considered to be quite stubborn. Since inflexibility is a common trait of people with OCD, they will almost always defer to rules and regulations without regard for moral or ethical considerations.

The under-belly source of a Wall personality is fear. They associate certain objects or situations with fear, and they learn to avoid the things they fear or to perform rituals that help reduce the fear. It is not uncommon for a Wall personality to have been raised in an extremely fear-based home or environment. The fear of doing "wrong", the fear of being judged and the fear of making a mistake can create deep tension and irrational, perpetual apprehension.

This pattern of fear and avoidance ritual may onset more so during periods of high emotional stress, such as starting a new school/job or ending a relationship. At such times, one is more vulnerable to fear and anxiety, but the Wall personality has a more difficult time pushing through these normal emotions. Things once regarded as "neutral" may begin to bring on feelings of fear. For example, a Wall personality who has always been able to use public restroom may, when under stress, make a connection between the restroom and a fear of catching an illness. Once a connection between an object and the feeling of fear becomes established, these types strictly avoid the things they fear, rather than confront, work through or tolerate the fear.

The Wall personality rejects anything unknown, and they have very poor negotiating skills because they do not want to hear from anyone else. They are the authority, after all. This fierce belief of control creates a rigid and stubborn personality. Their food selections can be obsessive and repetitive, often eating the same choices every day.

Justified: A police officer

Affected: Agoraphobic

7) <u>Predator (Parasite)</u>

Predators come in many forms and they can be classified by their intention. There are benign Predators, and there are malignant Predators. A benign Predator has minimal desire or intent to cause harm to another person, but they are fiercely programmed to win. These kinds of Predators thrive in business and sales. They love closing deals, starting and acquiring companies, winning a new customer and the like. They feel a sense of accomplishment when seizing control of other properties and entities. They differ from a Fire personality in that a Fire type is energy dominant – they thrive on being active and being viewed as a winner, whereas a Predator type seeks to seize and control other entities, always giving less than they receive.

A malignant Predator, on the other hand, will stop at nothing short of destroying the object of desire. They are incredibly dangerous, and typically classify as sociopaths. They use charm, manipulation, sexual attraction, intimidation and even violence in their means to control others. Once they obtain their sought after control, they use their victims to satisfy their own needs. They take what they want and they do as they please. The initial stage of manipulation is often incredibly charming, but it is merely a means to seize their prey.

Sociopaths are people characterized by a lack of empathy towards others that is coupled with displays of abnormal moral conduct and an inability to conform with the norms of society. Their desire to win overrides their willingness or ability to adhere to the rules and regulations of established communities. Earlier I discussed how this personality typically did not develop social awareness in early development. They learned to provide their own needs without awareness or compliance with their community. Other characteristics that sociopaths often display are stealing, lying, lack of remorse for others and/or towards living beings, irresponsible behavior, impulsive behavior, problems with the law, violating rights of others, aggressive behavior and so on.

The Predator personality is excellent at mimicking. Since they are completely removed from having emotions, they are fascinated in miming the emotions of others. They enjoy invoking emotion in others, satisfying their personal lack of feeling. They can successfully play other personality types as needed to seduce their victims (Fire, Sugar, etc). The difference will always be their lack of empathy and their desire to harm others -- they live for the win *or* the kill -- only this latter characteristic defines them as a malignant Predator. Both benign and malignant Predators tend to lavish fine food and human pleasures. Their diets often include large amounts of meat and animal products.

Justified: An entrepreneur

Affected: Serial killer

Everyone acts in dysfunctional ways, at least some of the time. Most everyone has felt emptiness and anger at one time or another. Who has never wanted to be the center of attention? Who has never been devastated when a relationship they were dependent on dissolved? People with personality disorders are not that different than people unclassified with one, as humans all have similar reactions to loss, abuse and injustice.

Those classified with personality disorders unfortunately have undeveloped stress management skills, less developed social skills and fewer possibilities for how to handle life experiences and situations. Whereas non-personality disordered people seem more able to communicate their feelings, are more flexible in their opinions, show greater decision-making skills and have a better time choosing the appropriate solutions to handle any given situation. Personality disordered persons too often fall back on their belief that they are incapable and that something is wrong with them, regardless of whether it is true or not. Non-personality disordered people are free to experience a variety of different states of mind, whereas those labeled with disorders tend to be limited to the same one, accumulated with obsessive repetition, until they literally are hypnotized into greater dysfunction that may onset or lead to a dormant illness or alter genetic formations.

As you review these types, you may resonate with characteristics of one or more. You are not defined by the characteristics or classifications. You life experiences to date have distinguished you in these ways. Every day is a new day. You have the control to shift your life and behaviors towards a more balanced state of being.

PART TWO

Chapter 5: Obtaining Dharma

The recurring patterns and synchronistic signs we experience throughout our lives can reveal a lot about our personal programming. They give us direct feedback as to how we think and what we are projecting. When you reach a state of realistic mirror awareness, you will be able to differentiate beyond any non-truth programming or experience. You will learn to navigate around anything that does not resonate as true.

The Dharma Zone program will guide you to states of health and consciousness -- mentally, physically and spiritually. It is designed to balance all personality types back to organic and realistic states of being. It will help a Sugar personality to find self-control, a Fire to know stillness, a Stuffer to learn self-care, the Airy type to discover realism, the Avoider to face reality, the Wall personality to soften their protective shells and a Predator to understand unity consciousness. Most everyone has qualities of each personality type, although deeper imbalances will lead one type to dominate. Once your subconscious mind is purified, your true, healthy self will be revealed again.

Although the program is designed for twenty-one days, the ultimate goal of The Dharma Zone is to initiate or refine a healthy lifestyle that will continue for the rest of your life. The longer you stay in this "zone", the sooner you will experience deeper levels of self-awareness and present-moment reality. This accumulative effect is the foundation of creating new healthy patterns for your healthy lifestyle.

There are specific behaviors that will keep you in The Dharma Zone:

- Avoid judgment

- Avoid blame (self or other)

- Remain non-reactive (including passive aggression)

- Have no expectations

As you follow this formula, your self-revelation process will naturally unfold. The process is polishing the mirror, so to speak. You are dong the work needed to reveal what is. *You* do not have to change, although your behaviors, fears and beliefs may. **Any** changes will be organic. You are not going to pretend to be something that you are not -- to the contrary, you will simply practice *being*.

Remaining non-reactive during the listening/witnessing phase will benefit you greatly. You are not always going to be happy with what you observe or how you feel. You are not always going to be comfortable. As you stop feeding unconscious patterns, unnecessary behaviors and untrue beliefs, they will begin dissolving away -- naturally. This is not unlike a nutritional diet. When we eat less, our true physical form reveals itself as any excess storage of fat is reduced to a normal level. With self-revelation, the practice of awareness *is* the change. It cannot be forced. It can only be realized.

I do believe that everything is perfect -- perfect according to our levels of consciousness or unconsciousness. Our minds are programmed very literally. Whatever lies in our subconscious will eventually find a way to manifest in our lives. Remember, dysfunction, too, will be formulaic and manifest "perfectly", as all manifestation does. What you think, what you feel and what happens in your life is always a match.

I often hear the refrain, "Everything happens for a reason." This can be quite the blanket statement of uncertainty and blind trust. Yes, everything does happen for a reason -- and that reason may very likely be a result of our poor conditioning and/or ignorant, self-defeating beliefs. Once we master control of our conditioning, in alignment with what is true, we will manifest conscious perfection – our dharma. It is then that we will discover the power to facilitate our destinies, and our abilities to have soulful, honest, functional and independent relationships.

When we are no longer ruled blindly by past programming we can begin manifesting realistic, positive, dharma-aligned programs. We will truthfully hypnotize ourselves, growing more connected to our true essence. It is at this point that everything in our lives will happen from intentional, natural and conscious choices instead of from ignorant, reactive and unconscious forces.

I encourage you to commit to this process. Commit to accepting each one of your challenges consciously, patiently and without judgment or attachment. Remember, no one is without his or her own challenges. Stay honest with how you feel, and give recognition to your feelings. No one is judging you, so there is no need for you to judge yourself. This is your time to sit with your reality and work it out.

Strong components of The Dharma Zone include relaxation, surrendering and unfolding. It is highly probable that you will experience a desire to *do* something or to move at times when you are to be observing stillness. The common reason for this angst is that we prefer to move, and we are accustomed to moving. You may find yourself seeking distractions and activities as a means to be relieved from being present. Underneath this desire for distraction are emotions and realities that may be uncomfortable, unprocessed or not exciting enough to keep your attention. We are either seeking pleasure or we are avoiding pain, and oftentimes a combination of the two. When we are uncomfortable in our current reality (oftentimes we are not aware of these discomforts), we look to shift attention away quickly. This is the crafty work of an affected ego to protect the shadow. Otherwise there would be fluid, peaceful transitions of present moment awareness leading into mindful activities.

Positive awareness ignites the manifestation process. With consciousness, we are able to apply positive energy to our innate desires, feeding our creative power. It is desirable and beneficial to be active, high frequency beings, but before we ignite the process of manifestation, it is imperative to remove any subconscious ignorance, energetic leashes and/or break down any internal dams we may have built. When the subconscious mind is pure, spontaneous manifestation happens instantly, without attachment, force or assisted substance control.

Celebrate every moment. Celebrate your limitations, challenges and unique differences. Express your true feelings, all the while adhering to Ahimsa, or Non-Violence. There may be times when deep feelings will bring up emotions such as anger or frustration. It is completely unproductive to your process to create deeper reactions, which will only add more negativity and karma to those emotional wounds. Do no harm to yourself or anyone else out of emotional anger, disappointment or grief. Nothing good will come from harming others. The past does not exist unless you carry the remains of it with you. Travel light.

The Dharma Zone is broken down into three phases:

Phase 1: Clear – The first phase of The Dharma Zone focuses on detoxifying the physical body. It is not only easier to sit comfortably in meditation when your body is in a state of balance, but it is also easier to witness your feelings with greater clarity. As you clear unnecessary patterns, beliefs, karmas and ignorance, it becomes easier to reinforce the self-hypnosis process of being you, as you are, according to the already present reality broadcasting through you.

In this phase, you will identify what you are naturally attracted to, as well as your personal, unique traits and preferences. You will begin discerning which of these desires and qualities feel organic to your dharma, and which ones are inhibiting it. Once you differentiate that which is real and that which is not, the practice of positive reinforcement will begin strengthening your I AM state of being, instead of subconscious ignorance weakening it. Repetitive practice is the road to success.

Taking the time to reverse deep-rooted beliefs that do not match your true dharma requires your full participation. Developmental programs feel comfortable – even when your expanded awareness realizes that they may not be healthy. When I was in college, working towards my degree in Child Development, I was required to complete an off-campus field study as part of my University's requirements. I chose to work for Child Protective Services. Part of my responsibilities included transferring children from their deemed unfit homes to their new foster homes.

The cases were often similar in nature. The current home situations were clearly toxic, confirming the hazardous environment concluded by CPS. Generally the homes were unclean; there were often signs of alcohol or drug use, and any adult guardians present appeared negative and aggressive.

I began the process by showing my credentials to the parents or guardians, followed by removing the child from their custody and home. After I strapped the child into the car seat waiting in the backseat of my car, I watched the child's reactions through my rear-view mirror as he/she assessed what was happening. Typically up until this point, the child did not cry or show any signs of resistance. Not until we arrived at a bright and clean foster home, that is -- with happy, positive foster parents waiting to embrace their new foster child.

It was at this point that the child typically reacted with fear and horror. All that this child had known was what he was raised with. He did not know or believe that clean, happy and positive attention was "better". Instead, he only knew that there was a sense of loss with what was familiar and known -- even if what he was losing was toxic and dangerous for his welfare.

Seek to understand the factors that have contributed to your personal development. Since you are reading this book, I would wager that you are taking control of your life; that you are willing to refine your developmental foundation as taught by your parents, guardians and environments. There may be areas of your life that were left undiscovered or uninvestigated that you may want to re-investigate today. You are now taking the time to apply positive, creative intelligence to all aspects of yourself needing attention and/or healing.

Much like our physical bodies, many of our attachments are necessary for our existence. For example, we have ligaments that attach of muscles to our bones. We need these to move with efficiency. We do not want to dissolve and detach beyond the point of healthy and necessary function. What we do want to dissolve and let go of are attachments that are holding our natural function back. Stagnation in our physical bodies, such as hardening in our lymphatic systems, circulatory systems, respiratory systems, muscular systems, skeletal systems and so on, affect our natural states of being.

When you let go of relationships, commitments and belief systems that do not align with your dharma, you are re-claiming your natural ranges of being. The Dharma Zone process will naturally repel people and situations in your life that drain you. You will no longer feed them, and they will no longer entice you. You can sit back and watch these shifts extending from your internal work. It would serve you, however, to understand why you wanted or needed them in your life to begin with. Thank each person or situation for filling the space that you once needed, and be ready to move on without any further attachment.

Phase 2: Be – In the second phase of The Dharma Zone you will focus on understanding who you are. You will seek to witness your true nature through the process of distilling and purifying. Stillness and non-reactivity is the focus and practice of this phase. The objective is to allow dormant, subconscious conditions to dissolve out of your psyche without reacting or resisting.

Your subconscious mind is like sand on a beach. In its pure state it is very impressionable. If you run a stick through the sand, it will leave a line. If the line was only a surface layer experience, the sand will heal itself and fill in the line. If, however, an experience is continually repeated, with reactive emotion adding strength to the line in the sand, the line will groove deeper and the sand will grow denser and less flexible. At these stages, it is more difficult to purify the subconscious – but it is not impossible.

Becoming conscious of your thoughts and feelings will reveal karmas (residual energies from past experiences). When you no longer feed these karmas (with reactive charge), the purification will begin. Self-knowing, self-acceptance and consciousness are all key practices in this phase.

It can be difficult to stay calm and detached as you re-play past events from your life, but remember that reacting literally re-acts the past drama, which is what we are trying to free ourselves from. Non-reaction – observing the reality and feeling the emotions without any form of reaction (action, distraction or emotional charge) will begin the process of liberation.

Phase 3: Reveal – The third phase of The Dharma Zone is self-actualization, the organic revelation of who you are. In this phase, the focus is on the I AM Process. By now, a deep sense of self-knowing is evident. You will now see visible rewards of your work. You may feel a deeper connection to yourself – as well as greater realization of who you truly are. "A-ha" moments will continue to increase in frequency. Having removed yourself from potentially limiting scenarios and people, you will feel more comfortable being yourself at home, at work and in your communities -- simply and confidently.

Distilled down to the most basic element, I AM is the utmost essence of being. It is the absolute power of who you are. The popular Sanskrit word Om is a form of I AM. There is no desire in I AM, for it is complete. There is no fear in I AM, because it is secure. There is no I AM fan page on Facebook, because it is detached from needing connection or approval. I AM has nothing to advertise because it isn't selling anything. It is void of ornamental or descriptive attachments. It simply is. Pure. Nothing added.

In this phase, a sense of self-power will become tangible. You will experience how your life begins unfolding perfectly from a healthy connection to yourself. You may realize how you previously functioned from a more forceful, disconnected and possibly desperate approach to your work and goals. Instead, you will now experience a timeless sense of self-control, power and presence – as if you have fully stepped into your life, filled with increasing awareness of all of your innate desires and dreams. That, which you need, will become present. Those, whom you seek, will appear. A natural flow of least effort perfection awaits you.

The Dharma Zone 21-Day Commitment

It is now time to unfold your truest you. The Dharma Zone guidelines are set up to help you get deeper into the Zone, but of course, it is completely up to you to adhere to them. If you deviate from the program, for whatever reason, simply start again. Consistency is far greater than the illusion of perfection. The "perfection" will result from your commitment to the process of self-awareness and self-care. Please, do not give up -- continue your efforts, as best you can. The program can be repeated as many times as you like.

Maintain a present state of realism while you are participating. Please do not think dramatic change will happen overnight, or be complete in twenty-one days. A pattern that took twenty years to form needs time, patience and consistent practice to be reversed. Even though you will see positive shifts, keep your focus on the journey. Commit to the healthy lifestyle, and commit to nurturing you.

The key to success is to show up and practice. If you become reactive, over-ruled by your emotions, or if you miss a yoga session, remember to show compassion to yourself. Most importantly, start again where you left off. Be honest with who you are – mistakes and all. Commitment, non-judgment and acceptance are highly valuable life lessons that will serve you well in life.

The Dharma Zone program guides you through twenty-one days of daily juicing, breakfast smoothies, salads for lunch, vegan soups, and an overall much lighter, less congesting food intake. First thing every morning, you will enjoy a lemon and ginger elixir with hot tea (honey or stevia are optional sweeteners). After your **Morning Walk**, yoga and meditation, you will enjoy your **Breakfast Smoothie**, with varying recipes every seven days (see Chapter 6 for daily **Recipes**).

This dietary menu and daily exercises of the program are designed to alkalinize your internal ecology, relax your energetic vibration, prepare your mind to focus solely on your present reality, and to begin the process of releasing untrue thought patterns. The menu consists of daily **Vegetable Juice**, **Salad, Vegetable Soup, Vegetable Side** and **Steamed Brown Rice or Quinoa**.

These are all phenomenal for alkalinizing your body. The menu will rotate weekly. The vegetable juices will consist of your choice of beets, spinach, parsley, carrots, kale, radishes, celery, cucumbers, cabbage, broccoli, ginger, spirulina and chlorella, combined with selected fresh fruit juices (mostly apple, lemon and mango) and additional super-food ingredients; all of which are phenomenal body detoxifiers. Feel free to improvise with the juice menus, as long as you keep the ingredients vegan, gluten-free and sugar-free, the quantities moderate and the choices healthy.

The program leads you through twenty-one days of movement, exercise and self-care treatments balanced with frequent periods of silence, contemplation, journaling and meditation. The physical exercises involve low-impact, full body movements, including twenty-one minute walks, yoga and meditation. You can follow yoga videos, DVD's or online classes, you can practice on your own, or you can go to classes in your community. The **AM Yoga** sessions should be more dynamic, flow classes (to your current ability) and the **PM Yoga** sessions should be more meditative, restorative deep stretching.

Likewise, your **AM Meditation** sessions should focus on the daily theme. For example: *I Am Creative*. As you sit for the specified amount of time, practice being creative. Feel creative. Mentally reflect on the inspiration included each day. The **PM meditation** sessions will focus entirely on non-reactivity. Choose a comfortable position (on a meditation cushion, chair or blocks). For the duration of time specified do not move. Simply witness each moment, as it happens. Witness yourself, as you are. Do not move, react, speak or allow your mind to wander away from the present moment.

Feel free to practice these exercises for longer periods of time – the minimum requirement is twenty-one minutes, but you are welcome to extend the durations to match your fitness levels (remember, moderation is queen). Relaxing, theta-frequency tones (without lyrics) played during these activities are beneficial to the process of awareness. During this time, viewing television, participating on social media sites, surfing the Internet and listening to music with lyrics is not advised. Music with lyrics or a strong beats are adding frequencies and information into your consciousness. Try to maintain as much silence in your home as you can.

You will have many liberties to go about your days as usual, assuming that you work full time. If you have the luxury of not working or caring to other projects or people for twenty-one days, please indulge in this program with deep self-focus and longer session times. There is no lesser benefit if you do work, but you may have to prepare more in advance to account for your schedule and responsibilities. When you find this commitment, the ritual becomes an effortless habit and lifestyle.

For the duration of the program there is a restricted meal plan. It is intentionally designed with minimally reactive ingredients. This is intended to calm any inflammatory triggers within your body, thus calming your overall physical and emotional frequency. Imagine an energetic frequency running through a puddle of water. When there is reactive energy, the water is chaotic, becoming cloudy and minimizing your ability to see clearly to the bottom. When your energetic frequencies are calm, you too will see more clearly into the depth of who you are.

Even if you do not show any sign of food allergies, dairy, animal products, most grains and processed foods still create reactive responses within the body, as do many other food choices that have been removed from The Dharma Zone meal plans. Food is a foreign substance that affects your body's states and responses; essentially, it is a drug. This program is simplifying what you are ingesting to keep the body's inflammatory responses as low as possible. It is very clean, natural and basic.

Aside from these dietary limitations, the biggest challenge may likely be not eating solid food after 8pm each night of the program. Not only will this help your body properly digest its food, it will help prevent the possibility of suppressing emotions with food. As we prepare for sleep, we begin slowing down. This is a common time to stuff the very emotions that we are aiming to liberate.

When the body is not digesting food, it is cleaning the rest of your body by digesting particles that threaten the overall health of your organism. If there is food in the stomach, the digestive process takes precedence, taking away from cleaning and repairing tissues. The greatest time for healing and internal self-cleansing is while you sleep. When you sleep with an empty stomach, you are helping your body to clean excess particles and restore healthy homeostasis.

It is helpful to lighten up any toxin intake by eliminating alcohol, coffee, cigarettes, refined sugars, processed foods/flours, saturated fats and chemical additives, all of which act as toxins in the body and are obstacles to your healing process. Stimulants and depressants alter your states for you. The ability to control your states without external aid is the ultimate power of self-control, and this is what we aim to strengthen. Animal products may carry an energetic memory from the animal – this too is interference. Prescription medicines from your medical doctors are absolutely allowed and advised. **Please consult with your doctor before making any changes in your health care programs.**

The largest deterrent to good health is stress, which triggers your body to release stress hormones into your bloodstream. While these hormones can provide the "adrenaline rush" to win a race or meet a deadline, in large amounts they create toxicity and slow down detoxification enzymes in the liver.

Every day you will have a daily intention, an "I AM" mantra. This mantra is a phrase to focus on being and practicing the attributes outlined for that day. Bring this book with you throughout the day as a reminder of what you are practicing, as well as to read the daily inspirations for each day. This accumulative process will plant the seeds of these positive intentions into your consciousness. You will inevitably see these seeds bloom in your life.

Become an ever-aware investigator of your own behaviors, life and consciousness. You will have thought provoking exercises to complete during the program. Write down your emotions in your journal along with your journal exercises. Each day of the program you will journal your **Mirror Theory** exercise. Share your honest feelings about the people that your attention focuses on that day. This could include your spouse, your parents, your children, your employer, your co-workers, your friends, and it could also include people you had never met before, or simply someone who caught your eye. They are symbols of your subconscious. You attracted them for a reason, and you will begin investigating how and why. Take note of how you feel around each person, rating your level of comfort to levels of discomfort. Please do not instigate conflict or excessive, selfless attachment. Simply observe. We are One. After you describe the dominant characteristics of these key players, follow by describing how those individuals symbolize parts of who you are. For example: I walked by my neighbor three times today, even though I normally see her once a month or less. Each time she really caught my attention. I know that she is recently married and she reminds me of how happy I felt when I first married Joe.

Your greatest power during this time will be your ability to witness and observe. Take note of everything that happens when you are silent and still. For example, who is the first person to call, what are they looking for, and what events occur that take you out of your stillness? Do you find yourself compulsively jumping to action for certain people or activities and not others? If so, which people and which activities? Those are the attachments that have the strongest hold on you, and the areas to focus your work on.

It will serve you best if you keep your social activity to a minimum during this program. Answer kindly, but limit the initiation of conversation – especially light, unnecessary chatter. Use your communication to obtain and inform others of necessary information, and to complete work requirements, but nothing more.

This self-investigation process will be most challenging for parents, and those caring for others. It is crucial to maintain care of your children while you are participating in The Dharma Zone, and a little practice is far greater than none. You may even be happily surprised at the gift you give your children by pulling back a bit of external control. You may watch your children grow into themselves a little more, allowing them to initiate conversation and activity.

Please make sure to monitor care and safety of any dependents that you are responsible for (children, pets, elderly).

Guidelines:

- Follow the vegan, gluten-free diet program
- Eliminate alcohol, sugar, cigarettes, coffee & recreational drugs, processed foods
- Do not eat any solid food after 8pm
- Daily low-impact movement: walking, yoga
- Avoid stress
- No television or movies
- No music with lyrics (theta tones and calming instrumental only)
- Do not initiate unnecessary chatter
- Daily Journal
- Daily Mirror Theory
- Practice present-moment awareness
- Drink a lot of water (preferably out of glass, not plastic)
- Be patient
- Be accepting
- Stay positive – find silver linings

What you will need

Aside from juice and meal ingredients (see Chapter 6 for Recipes), below is a list of what you will need:

- Walking Shoes
- Journal
- Yoga Mat
- Comfortable Workout Clothes
- Four 4-lb cartons of Epsom Salts
- Essential Oils (Lavender, Tea Tree, Rose)
- Dried Clay – facial mask
- Virgin Coconut Oil for cooking
- Virgin Coconut Oil as moisturizer
- Dry Skin Brush
- 8 oz. Finely Ground Coffee
- Hand Loofah Gloves
- Unpasteurized Apple Cider Vinegar
- Juicer
- Blender or VitaMix (recommended)
- Fresh Lemons
- Fresh Ginger

- Raw Honey

- Stevia

- Herbal and Green tea

- Jojoba Oil

- Seven bottles of Hydrogen Peroxide

- Brown Sugar

- Fleet Enema or Suppositories

- Raw Egg

- 1 can of unsweetened Coconut Milk

- 1 gallon Milk

- Tub for foot bath

- Bag of marbles (optional)

PHASE 1: CLEAR (Days 1-7)

The first week of the program is designed for you to focus on cleansing and detoxifying the physical body.

DAY 1

Intention: I Am Committed

At Waking: Lemon Ginger Elixir & Herbal Tea

AM Walk: 21 minutes

AM Y/M: 21-minute AM Yoga & 21-minute AM Meditation

Breakfast: Smoothie 1: Blueberry Pro

Lunch (12-2pm): Salad 1 & Vegetable Juice 1

Dinner (5-7pm): Steamed Brown Rice or Quinoa, Vegetable 1 & Soup 1

PM Walk: 21 minutes

PM Y/M: 21-minute PM Yoga & 21-minute PM Meditation

Treatment: Hot Epsom Salt Bath with Essential Oils

Mirror Theory: Write in your journal honest character descriptions of people who caught your attention today. How do you see yourself in these individuals?

Journal: 1) List goals and dreams that you've had since you were a child – list as many as you can remember 2) Recall times in your life when you did not finish a project or goal you intended to finish (list as many as you can remember). Next to each example, indicate why you did not finish. Fear? If so, what were you afraid of (succeeding, failing)? Was there a lack of desire? Laziness? See if you can find a common theme running through your list. Take note, also, if you greatly deviated from your childhood dreams. Do you still feel the life and hope of those dreams today? 3) How easy is it for you to commit to relationships, jobs, and/or projects? Write about the last time you felt a fear of commitment and/or an over-eager desire for a commitment.

I once heard that every symphony starts with the same note that it ends on. I am not sure how true this is in the classical music world, but it sure is motivating, even if it is only theoretical. Starting today, starting now, commit to living your life as the truest version of you. *How* you do things will matter more than *what* you do. Today's intention is *I Am Committed*. Commit to every action you take, whether it is driving your car, or preparing your food. Be in each activity. Commit to you. Commit to being honest with yourself. Commit to taking care of yourself. Commit to a healthy, happy life.

People who have the willpower to commit to something they want are the people who get it. People who are committed do not take discouragement seriously -- they do not give up. To stay committed, it is beneficial to continuously remind yourself of your goal: to reveal your true essence and purpose.

Your treatment for today is soaking in an Epsom salt bath. Floating has been proven to assist in relaxation. It is one of the most rapid and effective methods for getting into a deeply meditative state, as the entire physical body utterly surrenders. As the body reduces the amount of responses being fired (karmas, stress), you begin to witness the dissipating vibrations of past actions.

The qualities that arise from relaxation and stillness include: calmness, fluidity, intuition, non-attachment and spontaneous synchronicity – all of which induce an alpha state of mind. The alpha state of mind is a mental state of relaxed awareness. Typically this state is only achieved during meditation or while asleep and dreaming. However, humans can achieve this state while they are fully awake and functioning in the world.

The commitment to relaxation and "being" may feel antithetical at first. We tend to associate commitment with action, planning and force. Once you connect to the present moment, you will realize that there is much more going on here than past or future thoughts.

Many years ago I had an organic opportunity to show my commitment to myself. I married myself, actually. I walked into a wedding chapel at the Grand Wailea on the island of Maui. There were several women setting up flowers and arrangements. One of the women asked if I were the bride. I did not answer her as I continued looking around the chapel. She mistook my silence for a "yes" and began to give me a tour.

When we approached the altar, she left me for a moment to be in the space where my marriage would be officiated. I instinctually took that moment alone to partake in a mini-marriage ceremony to myself. I told myself that I loved me unconditionally, for better and for worse, richer and for poorer, in sickness and in health. As I walked out of the chapel, I noticed a woman selling toe rings outside. I bought two silver bands, placing them on at the top of my left ring finger, making my commitment ritual to myself official. I've been committed every day since.

Commitment builds character. It is fairly obvious to state that a completed task creates a sense of accomplishment. Each and every one of your accomplishments contributes to your overall routine of self-improvement. I personally do not think that there is anything more gratifying than knowing, accepting and living who we truly are. From this alignment, we have the power to attract everything that we need and desire.

"The irony of commitment is that it's deeply liberating -- in work, in play, in love." ~ Anne Morriss

DAY 2

Intention: I Am Creative

At Waking: Lemon Ginger Elixir & Herbal Tea

AM Walk: 21 minutes

AM Y/M: 21-minute AM Yoga & 21-minute AM Meditation

Breakfast: Smoothie 2: Sweet Green

Lunch (12-2pm): Salad 2 & Vegetable Juice 2

Dinner (5-7pm): Steamed Brown Rice or Quinoa, Vegetable 2 & Soup 2

PM Walk: 21 minutes

PM Y/M: 21-minute PM Yoga & 21-minute PM Meditation

Treatment: Dry Brush & Homemade Epsom Salt Scrub

Mirror Theory: Write in your journal honest character descriptions of people who caught your attention today. How do you see yourself in these individuals?

Journal: List ten or more creative projects that you have greatly enjoyed participating in throughout your life. Art? Writing? Fashion? Music? Building / Architecture? Design? Business? Cooking? Parenting? Film? Theatre? Teaching? Is there a common theme to your creativity? Write about what inspires you about these activities.

To tap into your innate creative nature, you only have to realize one thing: you are already a creator. You do not have to create exquisite paintings or breathtaking poetry. You are creating all the time -- simply by being alive. Every decision you make, every movement, breath, and word you speak, you are creating.

Sometimes, though, we can lose touch with that which our soul seeks to create – for many different reasons. Maybe you are using your creativity to fulfill the desires of other people? Or maybe a traumatic event or toxic relationship suppressed your ability to express yourself? Whatever the reason may be (if there is one) today's theme is centered on you expressing your unique creativity. "Perfect" does not exist, and you are the only creative director to listen to.

Remember, you do not have to be *artistic* to be creative. Creativity can be logical problem solving as well as personal expression of self through a project or performance – sometimes they can be both. The most important aspect to nurturing your creativity is to create – and to create frequently. Whether you create a new recipe for a meal, or write a letter to someone you have "feelings" for, or discover a faster route to your home from your office.

When you practice creating, you naturally get more involved in your life. You start to live more deliberately. Your everyday tasks become powerful and meaningful choices. You begin co-creating your life with your soul. Pay attention to everything around you, as inspiration lies in every moment. Be open to change, as Nature is continuously changing. Also, do not be afraid to explore pain or loss. Oftentimes the greatest creations result from life experiences that were most difficult and making something beautiful out of these heavier emotions can be very powerful. Be real. Be authentic.

Create Your Own Body Scrub

In addition to your journal exercises today, make a plan to create your personalized body scrub. Choose from the following ingredients: Epsom Salt, Lavender, Lemons, Oranges, Cucumbers, Ginger, Camphor, Honey, Castor Oil and/or Jojoba Oil. Choose your ingredients according to how you want the blend to affect you -- what qualities of these ingredients bring a sense of wellbeing and health to your senses? Include in your plan where to purchase the ingredients and with which proportions to blend them together. Your scrub will be used for today's Treatment.

"But, if you have nothing at all to create, then perhaps you create yourself." ~
Carl Jung

DAY 3

Intention: I Am Whole

At Waking: Lemon Ginger Elixir & Herbal Tea

AM Walk: 21 minutes

AM Y/M: 21-minute AM Yoga & 21-minute AM Meditation

Breakfast: Smoothie 3: Choco-co

Lunch (12-2pm): Salad 3 & Vegetable Juice 3

Dinner (5-7pm): Steamed Brown Rice or Quinoa, Vegetable 3 & Soup 3

PM Walk: 21 minutes

PM Y/M: 21-minute PM Yoga & 21-minute PM Meditation

Treatment: Facial Mask – Apple Cider Vinegar & Clay

Mirror Theory: Write in your journal honest character descriptions of people who caught your attention today. How do you see yourself in these individuals?

Journal: During your childhood, did you feel that your needs were provided for? This includes essential needs, such as food, shelter, water, clothing, and love. In addition to these essential needs, were your wishes and desires fulfilled, such as toy requests, trips, pets, etc.? Explain. Do you have anyone to thank or blame for this? If you do not feel that your needs and/or desires were fulfilled, it is time to give them to yourself. Today is a day of complete independence. Make a plan (from morning until night) to self-fulfill your needs and dreams. For example: 1) Upon waking, look in the mirror and tell yourself that you love you (sincerely mean it) 2) Prepare your morning elixirs, teas, smoothies and meals with love and wishes for great health 3) Enjoy your soul's company on your walks, meditations and yoga sessions 4) Get creative with the gifts you will give yourself today. When you feel a need or desire for something, make an independent plan to fulfill it. Expect nothing from anyone else.

Sometimes we can lose touch with what we truly need and want because we have grown accustomed to help or taking direction from others. To re-gain perspective and re-align with yourself, learn to listen to your needs and practice providing for them.

No man is an island, and we live in societies that participate together, but taking time to practice independence increases our appreciation for not only ourselves, but also for others. Ultimately, balance is the key. Being too independent could lead to a controlling, anti-social lifestyle, and being too dependent could lead to an uncontrolled, powerless lifestyle. Depending on others does not equate to weakness, nor does independence equate to strength. Seek balance. Seek healthy, complimentary partnerships.

Taking personal responsibility for your life also includes taking responsibility for any "mistakes" that may have occurred in your past. Even if your parents were not ideal, or you were the victim of misfortune at the hands of someone else, today you are letting go of blame or anger. The past is over. Today you are dealing with the cards in your hand only, and your plan is to make the best of what you are holding.

Remember, you are in control of your life. As you remove dependency from others, they may question your actions – maybe even condemn them. You do not have to explain your efforts to take care of yourself. Simply state that you are doing what makes you happy. If you ever feel your safety and welfare jeopardized when you take actions for yourself, please contact authorities for assistance.

It is wonderful to be alone, to be quiet. Actually, there is immense value in being able to think and act independently in a world of conformity and convention. In fact, all innovation and novelty depend on this. Each moment spent in self-awareness will add to your levels of self-understanding and self-realization. In the accumulation of these moments you will increase self-confidence, awareness and insight. You have all the answers inside of you. The more you trust yourself, the easier your life will flow.

"Promise me you will always remember -- you are braver than you believe, stronger than you seem, and smarter than you think." ~ Christopher Robin

DAY 4

Intention: I Am Forgiving

At Waking: Lemon Ginger Elixir & Herbal Tea

AM Walk: 21 minutes

AM Y/M: 21-minute AM Yoga & 21-minute AM Meditation

Breakfast: Smoothie 4: Pop-Eye

Lunch (12-2pm): Salad 4 & Vegetable Juice 4

Dinner (5-7pm): Steamed Brown Rice or Quinoa, Vegetable 4 & Soup 4

PM Walk: 21 minutes

PM Y/M: 21-minute PM Yoga & 21-minute PM Meditation

Treatment: Colon Cleanse

Mirror Theory: Write in your journal honest character descriptions of people who caught your attention today. How do you see yourself in these individuals?

Journal: Is there someone in your life that you are having a difficult time forgiving? A parent, friend, partner, ex-partner, abuser, betrayer? 1) On a separate piece of paper (not your journal), write down why you are upset with this person 2) Write down why you believe they took the actions they did that upset you 3) Safely burn the papers with a match or into a fire outside of your home. At the same time, peacefully escort this person out of your consciousness and say your final farewell. Holding anger inside only hurts you. Indifference is much more powerful and liberating than hatred. 4) Take control of your pain by healing where you feel injured. Be self-healing and self-loving.

*Please be mindful and safe near the fire you use to burn your list. *

By choosing to forgive the person who caused you pain (whether yourself or another), open your heart and *give* forgiveness. When we have been injured, a natural reaction is to self-protect. With that, we often stop giving, for fear of being vulnerable and hurt again. Sadly, this may lead to "holding on" to the negativity you felt was done to you, literally carrying it around with you. Have you ever seen a homeless person pushing a cart of their belongings that looks like garbage? This is what I picture when I witness others or myself clinging to past negative experiences. Circulating your emotions will help you to move on and travel light. If, however, you withhold the pain and stop giving, you are not only perpetuating the negativity, you are minimizing healthy circulation of energy.

Forgiveness is not letting an offender off the hook – it is merely freeing you of the negative experience, whether or not the "offender" is consciously sorry for their behaviors. You can and should still hold others accountable for their actions or lack of actions when they have wronged you. When it is time to move on, however, strengthen your focus on self-restoration and peace. No one else has to even be aware of your forgiveness. Everything you do you do for you.

"The forgiving state of mind is a magnetic power for attracting good."
~ Catherine Ponder

DAY 5

Intention: I Am True

At Waking: Lemon Ginger Elixir & Herbal Tea

AM Walk: 21 minutes

AM Y/M: 21-minute AM Yoga & 21-minute AM Meditation

Breakfast: Smoothie 5: Water Pro

Lunch (12-2pm): Salad 5 & Vegetable Juice 5

Dinner (5-7pm): Steamed Brown Rice or Quinoa, Vegetable 5 & Soup 5

PM Walk: 21 minutes

PM Y/M: 21-minute PM Yoga & 21-minute PM Meditation

Treatment: Gargle with hydrogen peroxide / Dental and mouth cleaning

Mirror Theory: Write in your journal honest character descriptions of people who caught your attention today. How do you see yourself in these individuals?

Journal: Are you comfortable sharing your thoughts, ideas and feelings with your friends? Is there some area or "story" in your life that is not honest? For example: "I dye my hair, but I don't tell anyone", OR "I present myself as the life of a party, but sometimes I feel extremely alone", OR "I lied about my work or school credentials", etc. Describe.

Defining truth can sometimes be tricky, as differing perspectives oftentimes come into play. The nuts and bolts of expressing truth looks like this: If one chooses to tell you what he is aware of, he is being honest. If one chooses to tell you something contrary to his awareness, he is lying. If one chooses not to tell you something that he is aware of, he is withholding.

Where truthfulness gets complicated is that we have the abilities to *believe* anything. The Emperor in the story, *The Emperor's New Clothes*, truly believed that he was dressed in fine clothing that only those who were superior could see. At first, out of fear of being inferior, he stated that he could see the fine linens the tailors had used for his suit (even though they did not exist). With repetitive reinforcement of this belief, the Emperor was soon convinced that he was indeed wearing clothes. Since he truly believed that his tailors were dressing him, he was not lying – but the reality is that he was not dressed.

In order to fully align with absolute reality and truth, we need to rely on our clear senses. We need to interpret each moment according to what we realistically perceive. We also need to bypass any programs in our minds that are not based on factual experiences. Ironically in *The Emperor's New Clothes*, it is a child who calls out to the Emperor that he was not dressed. Children have a much greater connection to truth. Before we are socialized to "belong" and "fit in" to groups, we simply say what we feel, think and see.

Throughout the day today, state factual comments, as you perceive them. For example: upon seeing an orange blanket, say "That blanket is orange", or while driving your car, say "I am driving my car", or when you feel tired, say "I am tired", etc. Since we have committed to Ahimsa during this program, refrain from vocalizing any negative or hurtful comments to yourself or others, even if you believe them to be true.

To avoid feeding negativity and reaction, speak from your current perceptions – not from past feelings. When you combine your experiences with your feelings, you will create a somatic memory program, which will begin attracting more of the same. You are working to dissolve unhealthy programs during this phase, not to create new ones. Holding unrealistic programs in your consciousness decreases your ability to perceive present and future experiences from an organic, truthful space. Have fun stating the obvious without emotional attachment everywhere you go today. *I Am True.*

"Our lives improve only when we take chances and the first and most difficult risk we can take is to be honest with ourselves." ~ *Walter Anderson*

DAY 6

Intention: I Am Unique

At Waking: Lemon Ginger Elixir & Herbal Tea

AM Walk: 15-30 minute

AM Y/M: 21-minute AM Yoga & 21-minute AM Meditation

Breakfast: Smoothie 6: Mango Pro

Lunch (12-2pm): Salad 6 & Vegetable Juice 6

Dinner (5-7pm): Steamed Brown Rice or Quinoa, Vegetable 6 & Soup 6

PM Walk: 21 minutes

PM Y/M: 21-minute PM Yoga & 21-minute PM Meditation

Treatment: Foot Scrub / Bath & optional Pedicure

Mirror Theory: Write in your journal honest character descriptions of people who caught your attention today. How do you see yourself in these individuals?

Journal: Write down everything what makes you unique -- your looks, your history, how you walk, your style, your experiences, your name, your philosophy, etc.

Despite advantages to belonging to a group or society, professional and personal success does not come from being generic. We often live our life pleasing others to maintain safety and to belong. This is how fashion and pop trends exist and rule. Most people whom I ask agree that skinny jeans and

116

ballet flat shoes are unattractive – yet, when this is the current style, this is what most of us will wear.

Oftentimes we place the way we look at ourselves in the hands of others. This can suppress our unique traits. If you want to be unique, stop trying to please others at your own expense and start doing the things that make you happy. You were given a beautiful, unique life. Trying to be something other than you is the greatest insult, not only to yourself, but also to the entire Universe.

You need to believe in your own perfect, unique self and capability to be exactly who you are. On a daily basis, every one of us are faced with countless choices. We can choose to follow the crowd or we can choose to listen to our own inner voice. Do not be afraid to have a sense of self. Soon others will be clapping for the simple and wonderful experience of you showing them the real you.

Throughout the day today, talk exclusively about yourself and your unique interests – without complaining, bragging or boring your companions. Feel confident that your unique-ness is interesting and worthy to share (which it is!). It may feel uncomfortable at first, but keep practicing.

"There is a vitality, a life force, an energy, a quickening that is translated through you into action, and because there is only one of you in all of time, this expression is unique. And if you block it, it will never exist through any other medium and it will be lost. The world will not have it. It is not your business to determine how good it is nor how valuable nor how it compares with other expressions." ~ Martha Graham

DAY 7

Intention: I Am Flexible

At Waking: Lemon Ginger Elixir & Herbal Tea

AM Walk: 21 minutes

AM Y/M: 21-minute AM Yoga & 21-minute AM Meditation

Breakfast: Smoothie 7: Anti-Ox Pro

Lunch (12-2pm): Salad 7 & Vegetable Juice 7

Dinner (5-7pm): Steamed Brown Rice or Quinoa, Vegetable 7 & Soup 7

PM Walk: 21 minutes

PM Y/M: 21-minute PM Yoga & 21-minute PM Meditation

Treatment: 30-60 minute Massage (optional 10 minute Sauna beforehand)

Mirror Theory: Write in your journal honest character descriptions of people who caught your attention today. How do you see yourself in these individuals?

Journal: Write down which areas in your life you feel rigid. With family, relationships, work, exercise, diet, planning, etc. What are your "deal breakers"?

Many times in my life, I have heard the following phrase, "Want to make God laugh? Tell him your plans". Since life rarely goes as planned, flexibility is essential in order to deal with the unexpected obstacles and opportunities that pop up in our lives. I do not believe that there is a person or being (God) who has completely mapped out every aspect of our lives – we would simply be pawns in a game. We do, however, come into existence with unique energies, purpose and free will that make us who we are and influence our path.

It is essential to have a plan, but it is equally essential to be flexible. Remember, your subconscious mind may not be perfect yet, and you may very well manifest experiences that are undesirable and that do not serve you or your purpose. Practicing flexibility will help you move around and through these experiences -- ideally without creating more undesirable consequences.

Additionally, not everything is in our control. We have formed communities and societies that are governed by rule and order. Being flexible and versatile is an advantage if you have the desire to live peacefully in society, as well as if you would like to succeed at your goals. You will experience day-to-day difficulties, delays and frustrations in your work and life and when dealing with other people. There are times when you have to deal with situations that do not fit in with your intentions or schedule.

It would be very frustrating to have worked hard towards a goal, yet have things still do not pan out as you hoped. Here is when the importance of flexibility comes in. Flexibility or adaptability is being responsive to change. It is the ability to continue with a changed situation or to modify when needed.

Without resilience, you may stubbornly hold on to things that did not work and continue repeating the same mistakes. Being rigid and inflexible will inevitably cause undue stress. There are far too many factors out of our control to be too rigid. Mental agility is also related to our perceptions, emotions, actions and motivations. A change in our environment, attitude or behavior can also influence how we think. When we're feeling happy or optimistic, for example, we tend toward broad and inclusive thinking. Fear or anger narrows our focus down to specific details. When we are able to make these mental shifts without remaining stuck in a particular mindset, we're demonstrating mental flexibility.

Review your list of where you are least flexible. Throughout the day, answer, "yes" to every *reasonable* request you are given today. For example: A co-worker asks you to switch shifts. If you have no scheduling conflicts, say "yes". Please do not say "yes" to any request that would make you feel unsafe, vulnerable or uncomfortable. At the end of the day describe how you felt being more flexible.

Be Willing to Change: Being rigid with yourself and your rules may indicate that you are resisting change to what you are comfortable with. Change is absolutely necessary for personal growth and success especially if what you have done before has not worked to your benefit. When you improve yourself, your world will change for the better.

PHASE 2: BE (Days 8-14)

During the **BE** phase of The Dharma Zone, your focus is centered on silence, awareness, acceptance and *being*.

DAY 8

Intention: I Am Accepting

At Waking: Lemon Ginger Elixir & Herbal Tea

AM Walk: 21 minutes

AM Y/M: 21-minute AM Yoga & 42-minute AM Meditation

Breakfast: Smoothie 1: Blueberry Pro

Lunch (12-2pm): Salad 1 & Vegetable Juice 1

Dinner (5-7pm): Steamed Brown Rice or Quinoa, Vegetable 1 & Soup 1

PM Walk: 21 minutes

PM Y/M: 21-minute PM Yoga & 42-minute PM Meditation

Treatment: Hot Oil & Coconut Milk Treatment for Hair and Scalp

Mirror Theory: Write in your journal honest character descriptions of people who caught your attention today. How do you see yourself in these individuals?

Journal: Sort through photographs from your childhood to present. Reflect on each phase of your life with self-love and gratitude. 1) Choose three photos that capture your essence. Write down what you remember about the time the photo was taken. Observe how happy, beautiful and lovable you are. Write a short note to yourself in those photos. Express gratitude to yourself for your beautiful essence 2) Choose one photo where you do not look the best (we all have them). Refraining from judgment, write a short note to that part of yourself as well. Express unconditional acceptance and gratitude. Frame one of your favorite photos of the three and place it in a visible location in your home.

One of the greatest challenges of The Dharma Zone process is accepting who we are, as we are, even while unraveling layers of karma and ignorance. No matter how distorted we seem from our source, true dharma can and will never die. It is our absolute essence. As we let go of any false beliefs, limiting attachments, fears and illusions, we will begin expressing ourselves from our authentic space.

When we express judgments and criticism (to self or other), they act much like reactions do. They scratch the grooves on our subconscious mind.

They are equally as hurtful to us as they are to others. Learning how to accept others and ourselves is healing for everyone. When a person who was about to judge lightens their aggression through acceptance, they realize how limiting their judgment was. The person who was victim to potential judgment may also soften their defense from the lack of attack – allowing their truth to emerge. This allows the opportunity for the relationship to blossom organically, regardless of difference.

Acceptance does not always have to indicate a relationship. Oftentimes acceptance of another person can be from a silent, loving distance. I have found it incredibly beneficial to stay clear of people who lack authenticity. I do not judge or label them; I simply accept them as they are, while focusing on my personal commitment to truth and integrity.

People judge for various reasons. Some have been raised in critical family environments, learning to judge others out of habit. Others judge as a projection of their own self-judgments; what they see in others is what they dislike in themselves. Some people have experienced trauma and have developed a negative perspective on life. There are many who use arrogance and belittling behaviors as a means to temporarily feel superior to others. And some people judge because they are highly intelligent, expecting a more advanced civilization. Their desire for something greater may result in frustration with the flaws of our current existence.

In the end, none of these tactics truly help a person to feel any better. While dishing out negativity to others, we have to carry it ourselves, and this is energetically toxic. The only way to find peace and love is through acceptance. The best place to start is by loving and accepting oneself. What we see if merely a reflection of who we are, therefore people who judge others are judging themselves. Remember, we're in this together. Those who feel good about themselves tend to see the good in others and be more accepting. It all starts within you.

Personally, I tend to focus heavily on truth in my relationships with others, and sometimes in my enthusiasm to tell the truth, I forget to be loving. I forget that truth is relative and less important than acceptance and love. Individual truths are subjective (not absolute truth, of course), but who am I to demand another individual to understand my level of truth comprehension? What I may be ready to hear and embrace, another may not yet be. Everyone has their own path, which is right and true for them. Just because we may not agree with how someone else lives their life does not mean that we have to change how we treat them. Acceptance takes precedence over truth, and the only ones we can truly change are ourselves.

Today, begin this journey of acceptance by releasing any judgments or regrets from past mistakes that you may have made in your life. Accept any flaws and scars that may have resulted. Focus on the absolute positive reality that you are a living, energetic being with a short opportunity to explore human existence – including the victories, the defeats, the love and the loss. With self-awareness and self-control, anyone can learn to shift their attention from a negative perspective to an uplifted, inspired viewpoint. It simply requires desire, awareness and practice.

"Real isn't how you are made,' said the Skin Horse. 'It's a thing that happens to you. When a child loves you for a long, long time, not just to play with, but REALLY loves you, then you become Real." 'Does it hurt?' asked the Rabbit. 'Sometimes,' said the Skin Horse, for he was always truthful. 'When you are Real you don't mind being hurt.' 'Does it happen all at once, like being wound up,' he asked, 'or bit by bit?' 'It doesn't happen all at once,' said the Skin Horse. 'You become. It takes a long time. That's why it doesn't happen often to people who break easily, or have sharp edges, or who have to be carefully kept. Generally, by the time you are Real, most of your hair has been loved off, and your eyes drop out and you get loose in the joints and very shabby. But these things don't matter at all, because once you are Real you can't be ugly, except to people who don't understand." ~ Margery Williams, The Velveteen Rabbit

DAY 9

Intention: I Am Patient

At Waking: Lemon Ginger Elixir & Herbal Tea

AM Walk: 21 minutes

AM Y/M: 21-minute AM Yoga & 42-minute AM Meditation

Breakfast: Smoothie 2: Sweet Green

Lunch (12-2pm): Salad 2 & Vegetable Juice 2

Dinner (5-7pm): Steamed Brown Rice or Quinoa, Vegetable 2 & Soup 2

PM Walk: 21 minutes

PM Y/M: 21-minute PM Yoga & 42-minute PM Meditation

Treatment: Hot Bath w/ Epsom Salts & Essential Oils

Mirror Theory: Write in your journal honest character descriptions of people who caught your attention today. How do you see yourself in these individuals?

Journal: In the morning, write down what events make you impatient. Describe how you feel when others delay your activities – for example: cutting you off in traffic or while you are standing in a line. Throughout the day today, allow others to go in front of you – while driving, waiting in line at the grocery store, etc. In the evening, write down how it felt to slow down and let others ahead.

It is not the words we say or the positions we take that define our truth existence. It is in calm, silent, unforced knowing that we are most true. Ideally, The Dharma Zone will instill in you an appreciation for process, practice and conditioning. This program is the ultimate commitment to yourself, and yes, it requires patience, but more importantly, you deserve patience.

The more attached to an outcome or situation that you become, the greater the chances of growing impatient when things do not go as you would like them to. Practicing non-attachment can help you become more patient during times of stress and/or excitement, both of which can greatly disrupt the natural flow of events in your life.

Being more patient generally requires learning new skills. One of the tried and true methods is learning to count to ten, especially before responding to a child or loved one in times of stress. Or waiting a day to respond to an email that made you see the color red. The goal is to allow the brain to catch up to our flight or fight response to extreme emotion. Choosing a brief pause, mentally or physically, helps us assess what is the healthiest approach to the situation, instead of reacting from our attachment and impatience. One can never unsay words that were spoken in haste. It is typically better to leave things unsaid until we regain control of the situation, our feelings and ourselves.

In other circumstances, we may need to build patience while we are waiting in lines, in traffic, or at the doctor's office, for examples. Waiting is often interpreted as negatively affecting our schedules for the day. This can quickly lead to anger, which may end up being projected at other drivers, employees, family members, and so on.

A change in your perspective about this unanticipated "waiting time" is to consider it a gift. The gift is that you get to spend quality time with the one and only, you. These are great moments for brief meditation, self-centering, breathing exercises, mantra, intention or prayer. Alternately, you never know if striking up a casual conversation with another person could prove rewarding, or if a delay could prove to your benefit.

The greatest key to being more patient is to alter the mind's perspective of "waiting" from an annoyance to a gift of repose. Cultivating a more patient personality can be incredibly rewarding. Suppose a conversation results in a friendship or a great business connection, or simply adds to the experience of being social. Maybe the traffic delay meant that you avoided an accident.

Try to see through unrealistic marketing schemes that offer a magic pill to fix your problems. Nothing of value comes without a bit of hard work and dedication, whether it is making money, building a home, having a healthy relationship or losing weight. Oftentimes it is the obstacles along our way that strengthen us to persevere in our goals. In our continued efforts (regardless of setback), we develop not only the strength to succeed and the personal belief in ourselves to be capable of victory, but we also *become* what we desire through the repetitive practice.

The trouble with patience is that when you need patience, you need it right now! Unfortunately, patience does not develop immediately. Patience must be exercised – repetitiously and continuously -- just like a muscle. Practice all day, every day, repetitiously, on the small stuff. It is these smaller examples that give us the opportunity to really exercise, develop and strengthen patience.

"Adopt the pace of nature. Her secret is patience."
~ Ralph Waldo Emerson

DAY 10

Intention: I Am Non-Reactive

At Waking: Lemon Ginger Elixir & Herbal Tea

AM Walk: 21 minutes

AM Y/M: 21-minute AM Yoga & 42-minute AM Meditation

Breakfast: Smoothie 3: Choco-co

Lunch (12-2pm): Salad 3 & Vegetable Juice 3

Dinner (5-7pm): Steamed Brown Rice or Quinoa, Vegetable 3 & Soup 3

PM Walk: 21 minutes

PM Y/M: 21-minute PM Yoga & 42-minute PM Meditation

Treatment: Hydrogen Peroxide Bath

Mirror Theory: Write in your journal honest character descriptions of people who caught your attention today. How do you see yourself in these individuals?

Journal: Are you comfortable in silence and non-doing? How do you seek to distract yourself when you are still? Do you seek the company of others? Food? Drink? Sex? Drama? How do you feel when you are in very quiet company? Throughout the day today, say nothing except in answer to questions which you are asked. At the end of the day, write down how this felt. Was it frustrating? Liberating? Explain.

As I mentioned earlier, the moments that we practice non-reaction allow the grooves on our subconscious mind to heal. On the other hand, each time that we react to similar stimuli, these specific grooves become deeper, resulting in the need for greater stimuli to feed it. This is the addictive patterning that we are looking to eradicate. The deeper the grooves, the longer the amount of sequential time needed in non-reactive stillness. No two people are programmed the same, therefore everyone has a different journey and healing path.

Our emotions often override our logic when we are being challenged with reaction feeding stimuli. Since you are not isolating yourself in a cave for twenty-one days, away from society somewhere, you may find some situations difficult to keep your cool. When you understand how reacting works to your disadvantage, you will most likely want to learn and practice the foundational skills of non-reactivity.

Imagine you are driving your car to work one morning. You are playing your meditation music on your car CD player. Just as you turn into the parking lot, you eye a car pulling out of a parking space. You bring your car to a stop and activate your blinker to indicate that you are entering the parking space as soon as it becomes vacant. Yet, as you are about to turn into the space, a car speeds around the corner and takes the space you were waiting for.

Before you can even open your mouth, the driver of the car looks you, rolls down his window, laughs out loud and turns off his car. You feel angry, surprised, and mistreated. Your body may even begin to tremble slightly, from the adrenaline. You are unable to do anything. You ask yourself, "What just happened? Why am I trembling?" In situations like this, we have the option to use our fight or flight mechanisms by attacking and/or raging. Since governmental laws of our societies discourage harm to others, we tend to implode our anger at ourselves or project it in smaller doses to those around us throughout the day. Yet, the other option in this situation is to become empowered.

The best way to avoid these types of situations is to never attract them in the first place. Remember that everything in your existence is perception. The Zen Buddhist would observe that experience simply as it happened. They would not perceive any personal injury. It was simply an experience, and they move on to the next. Non-attachment dispels the potential charge of emotion that attracts energy and drama. By not engaging your energy into those types of situations or people, you greatly lessen your chances of creating more karmas. The harder the situation is to remain non-reactive, the stronger you will ultimately become.

It is useful to understand not only what was happening in the example above, but also what is the best way to build your inner emotional strength of non-reactivity. If you've experienced a situation like the one I described, then you probably know the feeling when negative energy throws your entire energy system into a state of frustrated chaos. This can happen in any type of heated argument; at work, with family, and any of our intimate relationships. In moments like these, we can become overpowered by the external situation – left feeling confused, energetically and even physically drained.

How can we maintain a state of being so that outside negativity does not create an imbalance within us? How do we maintain our personal power and organic dharma? As I mentioned, what most of us do in these situations is to become reactive. Fight or flight. Some will fight back, some will run and others will give in (maybe with internal fury). Instead of becoming reactive, a good alternative is to calmly state the reality of the situation at hand. Your balanced state will outlast their outburst. How do we achieve this balanced state? One way is through an energy technique to redirect your energies for something productive – I call this "Use It".

When we are emitting emotions, the central energy pathway, or meridian, which governs our central nervous system functions like a radio receiver. It will emit signals of your thought and sensory vibration. These signals will attract similar energies, so it is best to utilize the power for something productive and good (instead of destructive and negative). The energetic charge that you receive is a gift. Using this charge productively is entirely up to you.

The central meridian runs from your pubic bone up to the crown of your head. You can use the electromagnetic energies of your hands to gather the energy brewing in your CNS and "use it" for something positive (new job, love, health, world peace, etc.) By consciously pulling your hands up the central meridian, you are able to draw protective energy along the meridian line while guiding it to your positive intention. This is the natural direction that the central meridian flows. By moving with it in this manner, you are able to connect with and utilize this energy.

While "using it", breathe deeply. You will begin to feel centered and in control of your emotions and reactions. The energy from your hands radiates an electromagnetic force. The central meridian is also closely tied to our thoughts and feelings, which makes it very responsive to self-hypnosis. A powerful way to instill affirmations such as "I AM non-reactive", "I AM healthy", "I AM loved", etc. is to simply state them in your mind and heart while you are "wishing" the energy with your hands. As you continue to practice this level of awareness and witness, you will be less affected by your emotions, and even of those around you.

Learn to Deal with Difficult People and Situations.

You cannot change events and people, but you can adjust and modify your own behavior and habits. You may have to learn to communicate and influence others more effectively. You may also need to look at your own attitude on how you judge and perceive others and things.

"Although attempting to bring about World Peace through the internal transformation of individuals is difficult, it is the only way." ~ Dalai Lama

DAY 11

Intention: I Am Aware

At Waking: Lemon Ginger Elixir & Herbal Tea

AM Walk: 21 minutes Walking Meditation

AM Y/M: 21-minute AM Yoga & 42-minute AM Meditation

Breakfast: Smoothie 4: Pop-Eye

Lunch (12-2pm): Salad 4 & Vegetable Juice 4

Dinner (5-7pm): Steamed Brown Rice or Quinoa, Vegetable 4 & Soup 4

PM Walk: 21 minutes

PM Y/M: 21-minute PM Yoga & 42-minute PM Meditation

Treatment: Baking Soda Bath

Mirror Theory: Write in your journal honest character descriptions of people who caught your attention today. How do you see yourself in these individuals?

Journal: How do you deal with stress or discomfort? How do you respond to stressful experiences throughout the day? Example: I ran late for my bus – my face appeared frantic, I looked disheveled and I was embarrassed when I got onto my bus.

As I trust that you know, our lives are short. We only have a very finite amount of time to gain self-awareness. Yet, without having self-awareness, the concept is difficult to understand. We can increase self-awareness through experience and a focused concentration on our experiences. Our minds are generating thoughts and perceptions nearly every moment of our lives, yet some people are not aware of this.

One of the best ways to increase self-awareness is to listen to and understand your own mental chatter. Mental chatter (or self-talk, internal monologue, voice of judgment, among other names) is the voice in your head that is constantly running in your mind. The mind often repeats the same thoughts over and over again, like in a loop or a record that got stuck in a groove. If these are positive thoughts, this can be very productive (albeit limiting), but all too often these are negative thoughts or a negative mental images that intensify stress, worry, anger, resentment and/or frustration. These are thoughts that are destructive and detrimental to your health and wellbeing.

Comparing mental chatter with how people answer the question, "What are you thinking?" helps to illuminate what is truly being generated in the mind. You might say "I'm thinking about what to eat," but your mental chatter may sound more like this:

> *I'm hungry… what should I eat?… is it 1:00pm yet?… shoot, it's only noon, it's too early to eat now… but I'm hungry… geez, I have been eating a lot lately… maybe I should go on a cleanse like Megan… she looks great… if I make it another hour it'll be OK… maybe I'll just*

have a salad… I'm horrible at controlling my diet… my mother was

right…. I better work out after work today… I need to get an x-ray of

my knee – it's still acting up… maybe I should just do yoga… that'll

be good, I'll do yoga… then I can eat early… is it 1:00pm yet?…

And it probably goes on and on as such. If you can get a clear read on what your mind is generating you can learn some great insight on how your mind is programmed. This example of chatter illustrates a person who possibly 1) was shamed by her mother about her weight 2) compares herself to her peers 3) is critical of herself, to name a few possibilities.

Learning to control and manage your mental chatter is one of the most fundamental elements to improving your life, because as we have learned already, our minds will create and attract scenarios according to the thoughts that we generate. Awareness of your mental chatter is the foundation to managing your life.

One of the key points to detaching from the mental chatter of the mind is to shift our point of view to details of the present moment. This is not something that we can think our way into doing – you simply have to let go of past experience and future expectations to immerse yourself in the *now*.

In times of stress or discomfort, do you ever seek distractions and external comfort? If so, how? Eating, drinking, drugs, work, sex, sport? Spend twenty minutes or more journaling about these behaviors and reactions. Bring your
150

journal with you today. Write down your feelings throughout the day, as well as how you respond to these feelings. Be mindful not to shame or judge yourself. Factually list your truthful feelings and behaviors as if you were a doctor, scientist or detective examining factual evidence as a means to greater understanding.

Anything we do can become meditative, including eating, driving, washing, cleaning the house, and, of course, walking. Walking meditation, also called mindful walking, combines the basic principles of meditation, such as breathing, concentration and relaxation with rhythmic walking. Be mindful of each step. Allow yourself to notice your surroundings, such as grass, trees, chirping birds, and the sun on your face. To end the walking meditation, gradually come to a stop, and become aware of the feeling of standing still again. Notice how you feel now, compared to how you felt when you started. Take your newfound awareness and calm with you for the rest of your day.

"Walk as if you are kissing the Earth with your feet." ~ *Thich Nhat Hanh*

DAY 12

Intention: I Am Authentic – As I Am

At Waking: Lemon Ginger Elixir & Herbal Tea

AM Walk: 21 minutes

AM Y/M: 21-minute AM Yoga & 42-minute AM Meditation

Breakfast: Smoothie 5: Water Pro

Lunch (12-2pm): Salad 5 & Vegetable Juice 5

Dinner (5-7pm): Steamed Brown Rice or Quinoa, Vegetable 5 & Soup 5

PM Walk: 21 minutes

PM Y/M: 21-minute PM Yoga & 42-minute PM Meditation

Treatment: Lemon and Honey facial

Mirror Theory: Write in your journal honest character descriptions of people who caught your attention today. How do you see yourself in these individuals?

Journal: 1) Describe your authentic self 2) Make a list of what you are attracted to 3) Describe how you think others perceive you 4) List your "Naysayers" 5) List those whom you feel most "you" around 6) Express yourself authentically

There is little more refreshing than encountering someone who is the same on the outside as they are on the inside. It is effortless and attractive. To the contrary, a person who's outside deviates from their inside can be draining and confusing, to say the least. One of the first steps to being authentic is to be true to your self. If you are a "people pleaser", you may have a more difficult time being authentic than those who take action from self-knowledge and direction. Knowing what *you* want is much more difficult if you are accustomed to deferring to someone else's wishes and/or looking for validation from others.

1. **Describe your authentic self:** How would you describe yourself? This aspect of you is not defined by your occupation, relationship, function or role. It is your core being. It is what makes you unique. It is not who you have been told that you are, nor is it what you are supposed to be and do.

2. **List what you are attracted to:** What do you love about yourself? Who do you love to spend time with? What brings you passion and joy? What makes you uncomfortable? What leaves you feeling uneasy or bad?

3. **Describe how you think others perceive you:** How do you think other people in your life perceive you? Who does your family think you are; your friends, co-workers, neighbors, etc.? How close are they to how you have described yourself.

4. **Identify the Naysayers:** List the people in your life who do not support you as your authentic self. Sometimes it is those closest to you who are not in support of you.

5. Identify those whom you feel most "you" around: List the people in your life who you feel most comfortable and most authentic around.

6. Express yourself authentically: Do what you say. Be who you are. Start listing ways in which you can feel more "you" around those groups or individuals who may not perceive you as you perceive your authentic self.

As you gain greater insight to who you are and what you enjoy, it is liberating to free yourself from any dysfunctional people in your life. No one can control you against your will, nor do you have the ability to change or control someone else. As you identify the people and things that leave you feeling untrue, remind yourself that you cannot change that. You cannot make someone else feel differently about you, so save your power. Let go of whatever makes you feel misaligned, untrue or "bad". Do more of those experiences and surround yourself with people that leave you feeling good and true.

Authentic people act from their intrinsic motives. Their thoughts, beliefs, words, and actions originate from within; they are true and secure enough to resist destructive external pressures. The result is a genuine, revitalizing and peaceful confidence that is void of anxiety, self-doubt, or stress.

"There is nothing more beautiful than seeing a person being themselves. Imagine going through your day being unapologetically you." ~ *Steve Maraboli*

DAY 13

Intention: I Am Consistent

At Waking: Lemon Ginger Elixir & Herbal Tea

AM Walk: 21 minutes

AM Y/M: 21-minute AM Yoga & 42-minute AM Meditation

Breakfast: Smoothie 6: Mango Pro

Lunch (12-2pm): Salad 6 & Vegetable Juice 6

Dinner (5-7pm): Steamed Brown Rice or Quinoa, Vegetable 6 & Soup 6

PM Walk: 21 minutes

PM Y/M: 21-minute PM Yoga & 42-minute PM Meditation

Treatment: Dry Skin Brushing & Sugar Scrub

Mirror Theory: Write in your journal honest character descriptions of people who caught your attention today. How do you see yourself in these individuals?

Journal: Focus on a few goals at a time each week. Log them, keep a journal and keep track of your progress. Not only will this help keep you motivated, you will also be able to track your success. Please list your short-term goals for this week.

We become that what we repeatedly do. There really aren't many intricate tips or tricks for staying consistent on the road to success other than being consistent. We do not need to complicate the matter, really, because staying consistent is incredibly simple – take action. It is completely normal to have days when we don't want to study, practice or work — this feeling isn't unique to anyone. Yet, consistent practice is the foundation for success.

Think about it -- it took consistent action to get you into the routine of who you are today. Where you are today -- be it career, relationships, weight, body image, finances, etc. -- was not an overnight occurrence. It took consistent action of doing the things that ended up serving (or not serving) you in the long run. The old adage, "Practice makes perfect" is only a half-truth if you are practicing something that isn't right for you.

A large part of the problem of inconsistency is unrealistic expectation. We are human beings with feelings. Emotions and external factors can sometimes get in the way and we can't always follow an exact routine. This should not stop us from developing discipline, though. Discipline takes time to develop and every journey has a first step. The best advice to becoming more consistent is simple: 1) Do something 2) Do it on a regular basis.

Many people associate consistency with boredom and possibly even a lack of initiative or creativity. Some people think that if something isn't improving after a few weeks or months that you need to change it. Yet, it could be this attitude that is keeping you from completion of a goal. Surprisingly, doing something every day or nearly every day is far easier to sustain than doing it once in awhile. If you want to be consistent with a new habit, run it every day uninterrupted for a month. Make it an irreplaceable part of your life, not an afterthought you do occasionally or when you feel that you need it. Inevitably, you cannot do something every day -- but you can at least make it work on a fixed schedule, for example: once per week, but *every* week.

Do you remember the sitcom, *Gilligan's Island*? It would not have been as entertaining to watch if the stranded status of the crew was remedied. Yet, what if Gilligan and his gang actually tried the same, previously failed tactic to get off the island once again? What if during the second attempt to execute their plan Gilligan did not accidentally trip over the rock, or extinguish their fire signal (which had previously sabotaged the near successful escape from the island)?

The evolutionary persistence towards success I am referring to is defined as continued diligence with improved and modified actions resulting from your experiences. Consistency is the foundation of practice, and practice is the foundation for success.

If you are having difficulty managing your current workload or your daily schedule, then you need to adjust it until it is something that feels right for you. Create a lifestyle that is fulfilling, rewarding and custom-designed for your needs and goals.

"We are what we repeatedly do. Excellence then, is not an act, but a habit." ~
Aristotle

DAY 14

Intention: I Am Present

At Waking: Lemon Ginger Elixir & Herbal Tea

AM Walk: 21 minutes

AM Y/M: 21-minute AM Yoga & 42-minute AM Meditation

Breakfast: Smoothie 7: Anti-Ox Pro

Lunch (12-2pm): Salad 7 & Vegetable Juice 7

Dinner (5-7pm): Steamed Brown Rice or Quinoa, Vegetable 7 & Soup 7

PM Walk: 21 minutes

PM Y/M: 21-minute PM Yoga & 42-minute PM Meditation

Treatment: Foot Reflexology Session

Mirror Theory: Write in your journal honest character descriptions of people who caught your attention today. How do you see yourself in these individuals?

Journal: As you go through the day today, see how quickly you can perceive an experience and let it go. Practice increasing the time between your perceptions of each experience. This is not a race, and it is not better to be faster, but you are training your awareness to stay present. At the end of the day, re-cap your day of being present. How did it feel to "let go" of perceptions to move to the next moment? Did it feel natural? Challenging? Unresolved? Refreshing? Describe.

To be aware is to be mindful – both of which indicate that you are fully present in each moment. When you are present you are aware of as many reality-based aspects of your moments as possible -- including your thoughts, feelings, actions and reactions. This also includes everything in your sensory stimuli, for example: what you see, what you hear, what you taste, what you smell, what you are touching and what you are feeling. You are paying attention to everything around you, as it happens. With increasing self-awareness you will notice how you interpret, perceive and respond to each bit of stimuli in each moment.

Mindfulness is our natural state of being. Watch your pets. They may have conditioning, but they are still present because they have not attached emotions or expectations to past or future events that inhibit them from experiencing each present moment.

Being present challenges the belief that the best way to become effective is to refer to the past and the future. The practice of awareness instead purports that only in the present moment experience can we accurately observe and describe what is truly happening, thereby being most effective and successful. This practice also contends that if we "listen" to each moment, our "inner knowing" or higher truth has a greater probability of being heard, guiding us to serve our most true interest, or dharma.

Much of our everyday experience is influenced by projections that we put on to the people and things around us. In other words, we're not seeing things clearly because we are projecting past experiences on to the new present. How often do you notice when you're projecting in this way? There are many benefits to being present. You will have greater focus, be less reactive, make clearer decisions, be more patient and have greater listening skills.

Notice the little improvements along the way. Be mindful that, no matter how frustrated, disappointed or angry you may become in a given moment, all things arise to pass away. All things will eventually change. This includes emotional "highs" as well (happiness and joy). Strive to live a life of balance, realistically appreciating your continually increasing awareness and evolution.

"When one door closes another door opens, but we so often look so long and so regretfully upon the closed door, that we do not see the ones which open for us."
~ Alexander Graham Bell

PHASE 3: REVEAL (Days 15-21)

During the **REVEAL** phase of The Dharma Zone, your focus is centered on the revelation process of self-creation. You will begin defining who **I AM**.

DAY 15

Intention: I Am Energy & Light

At Waking: Lemon Ginger Elixir & Herbal Tea

AM Walk: 21 minutes

AM Y/M: 42-minute AM Yoga & 21-minute AM Meditation

Breakfast: Smoothie 1: Blueberry Pro

Lunch (12-2pm): Salad 1 & Vegetable Juice 1

Dinner (5-7pm): 1 cup steamed Brown Rice or Quinoa, Vegetable 1 & Soup 1

PM Walk: 21 minutes

PM Y/M: 21-minute PM Yoga & 42-minute PM Meditation

Treatment: Acupuncture Session

Mirror Theory: Write in your journal honest character descriptions of people who caught your attention today. How do you see yourself in these individuals?

Journal: When you experience yourself in stillness, you will increase your connection to your energy and soul. Write down who you are. Let your answers start with "I AM". Let your answers flow naturally – there is no right or wrong. Your statements will not permanently define or label you; they are mere expressions of your soul in this moment.

After two weeks of The Dharma Zone program, I would believe and hope that you are feeling lighter -- physically, mentally and emotionally lighter. To be able to heal ourselves, we need to understand that the Universe is made entirely of energy. Likewise, the physical world, or the manifest Universe, is not made of solid matter, but of energy. Time and space are the dimensions along which energy moves, and everything (and everyone) we know is composed of energy.

Yogis, too, have believed in energy systems running throughout our bodies. These energy centers, or "wheels", are called chakras. Each chakra vibrates at a different frequency, creating different colors and sound tones. In addition, each chakra co-exists with a major organ or gland of the body. It is the output energy from these systems that creates the chakra. For example, the heart center vibrates at a different frequency than the brain center emits. In

170

order for our bodies to function at their greatest capacity, it helps to keep our chakra systems clear so that our energies stay free of congestion.

What is called life energy is, in fact, electromagnetic energy that we absorb from the Universe, Earth and our greater environment. We receive charge to our energy systems from interactions with our environment, including the people around us, from the air we breathe and from what we eat and drink.

Everything that you do, think or say emits an energetic vibration, which resonates with anything around you that is of a similar vibration. You are constantly creating yourself at every moment and sending your signals of "I AM" to the Universe, which will match your signal. As you become increasingly aware of every signal that you create (thought, action, word, emotion), you will notice how these signals form your experiences and existence (individually and collectively).

We are all made from the same Source Energy, whether you call that Source God, Buddha, Allah, Goddess, Universe, or Love. We have inherited all the power and knowledge that belongs to Source, but sometimes we forget that we hold this great power.

As you begin re-connecting directly to your higher truth and innate intelligence (Source), you will feel an increased natural energy and lightness. You may find great relief in this connection, as it is free from high and low fluctuations, judgments, conditions and "worldly" pressures that our societies have created.

Being Light & Love by Mother Teresa

People are often unreasonable, illogical, and self centered. Forgive them anyway.

If you are kind, people may accuse you of selfish, ulterior motives. Be kind anyway.

If you are successful, you will win some false friends and some true enemies. Succeed anyway.

If you are honest and frank, people may cheat you. Be honest and frank anyway.

What you spend years building, someone could destroy overnight. Build anyway.

If you find serenity and happiness, they may be jealous. Be happy anyway.

The good you do today, people will often forget tomorrow. Do good anyway.

Give the world the best you have, and it may never be enough. Give the world the best you've got anyway.

You see, in the final analysis, it is between you and God. It was never between you and them anyway.

DAY 16

Intention: I Am Joyful

At Waking: Lemon Ginger Elixir & Herbal Tea

AM Walk: 21 minutes

AM Y/M: 42-minute AM Yoga & 21-minute AM Meditation

Breakfast: Smoothie 2: Sweet Green

Lunch (12-2pm): Salad 2 & Vegetable Juice 2

Dinner (5-7pm): 1 cup steamed Brown Rice or Quinoa, Vegetable 2 & Soup 2

PM Walk: 21 minutes

PM Y/M: 21-minute Gentle Yoga, 42-minute PM Meditation

Treatment: 30-60 minute Massage (with optional 10 minute sauna beforehand)

Mirror Theory: Write in your journal honest character descriptions of people who caught your attention today. How do you see yourself in these individuals?

Journal: Are you comfortable being happy and joyful? Do you feel you have to cling to disappointment to protect yourself from falling into it? Is it easy to compliment other people? Is it easy to whole-heartedly share their successes and joys? Do you find emotions like jealousy or anger arise when others are happy? Did your parents allow you to be happy as a child? What makes you happy? How do you feel and act when you are happy? Describe.

While we may have different life goals, there seems to be an almost universal underlying goal to virtually all pursuits: the goal to be happy. People who want financial wealth generally do so because they believe that the money itself will make them happy. People strive for the perfect relationship, the perfect house, the perfect body, and the approval of others, all in an attempt to be *happy*. Sometimes these things do make us happy. Sometimes, however, we create unnecessary stress in attempts to reach these desired goals that we feel will bring happiness. Or, we may reach these goals only to find that we're still not happy.

More importantly than your lifestyle and possessions, your attitude about life and the things that happen to you each day can also greatly impact your overall level of happiness and life satisfaction. I do not think it is any secret that optimists tend to be happier people, but you may not realize that there's more to optimism than 'putting on a happy face' or 'looking on the bright side of life'.

Cultivating the mind of an optimist often means cultivating happiness, regardless of your circumstance, and it typically brings more things into your life to be happy about (The Law of Attraction). Remember, happiness in itself is great wealth. It is the abundance consciousness that will attract more of what you desire – be that financial wealth, love or other.

In addition to optimism, happy people tend to have an internal control center; they tend to believe that they are the masters of their fate, rather than the victims of circumstance. Regardless of what is happening, they can control how they feel. When you view the stressors of your life as a challenge rather than a threat, you will more likely seek a victory instead of falling in defeat.

The difference between happiness and joy is subtle. Whereas happiness depends on a circumstance, joy is part of your true nature and does not fluctuate based upon what happens in your life. It is a steady constant. Expressing Joy is empowering. Expressing joy helps you feel more confident and comfortable about who you are. It is energetically and physically healthy to experience joy, through your speech, actions, or artwork.

How to embrace joy into your life:

Make Happiness a Priority. Sit down and think about all the things that are wonderful in the world. I never heard of anyone on their deathbed saying, "Gee, I wish I had sold 50,000 more paintings." Happy people aim to be happy, and they work at it. They pursue their interests.

Say goodbye to inner and outer critics. Negative self-talk inhibits self-expression. For example, if you say, "I can't" or "I'm not good enough, fast enough, strong or young enough," too often, that is exactly what you will be. Stay clear of *happiness bubble-busters* -- people who are critical of you and your goals, and who do nothing but complain or discourage you. Release all those limiting thoughts and people that hinder you from being happy. Do what makes you joyful.

Embrace Imperfection. Not every creative expression in life is going to be a first-place effort. While you are learning to let your light pour out, it may be a little uncomfortable at first. Keep going, keep practicing, and keep dancing. *You are living art.* Smile a lot.

Live from Your Heart. Let go. Joy and creativity are right brain, intuitive processes. Do not worry about how you look -- just keep shining your light.

"What I know for sure is that you feel real JOY in direct proportion to how connected you are to living your truth." ~ *Oprah Winfrey*

DAY 17

Intention: I Am Grateful

At Waking: Lemon Ginger Elixir & Herbal Tea

AM Walk: 21 minutes

AM Y/M: 42-minute AM Yoga & 21-minute AM Meditation

Breakfast: Smoothie 3: Choco-co

Lunch (12-2pm): Salad 3 & Vegetable Juice 3

Dinner (5-7pm): 1 cup steamed Brown Rice or Quinoa, Vegetable 3 & Soup 3

PM Walk: 21 minutes

PM Y/M: 21-minute PM Yoga & 42-minute PM Meditation

Treatment: Coffee Body Scrub

Mirror Theory: Write in your journal honest character descriptions of people who caught your attention today. How do you see yourself in these individuals?

Journal: Write a letter to the "creator" of the Universe (whether you believe it to be a being or scientific force). Thank the Universe for your life. Be specific as to details you are grateful for and how they came into existence in your life.

Cultivating and practicing gratitude can reduce symptoms of mild to moderate depression and anxiety – resulting in better mood and sleep. Practicing gratitude can also lead to increases in optimism, vitality, happiness, a sense of wellbeing, and a greater satisfaction with life. Grateful people tend to be more forgiving and more likely to help other people in need. Grateful people also appear less envious and more generous with their possessions. This naturally facilitates better quality relationships. Gratitude also helps in coping with adversity. Those who practice thankfulness in times of adversity are more likely to seek and find a "silver lining" in their experiences.

Keep a Gratitude Journal

Record daily five blessings or gifts you have felt or experienced, such as your career, good health, a positive relationship, improvements at home, or lessons learned. Describe the experiences, and write down your thoughts and emotions about them (rather than merely itemizing them). Your purpose is to build your sensations of gratitude, which will encourage you to experience it more often.

Think about someone who has been kind or has done something for you whom you have never properly thanked. Consider, for example, parents, grandparents, friends, teachers, coaches, and employers. Write that person a gratitude letter, being specific about the details of the kindness toward you and how it affected you.

Eliminate Ungrateful Thoughts

Identify and list any internal complaining and ungrateful thoughts. Find the silver lining in each situation and replace the negativity with grateful thoughts and problem-solving strategies. We are prone to be more grateful when we focus on positive action rather than passive complaining.

Train Yourself to Be Grateful

Make gratitude a habit. Say 'thank you' frequently to your loved ones – a well as to cashiers, customer service agents, postal workers, and others who serve you in any capacity. Far too many people go through their lives without having ever explored the great gift that they were given – their life. This includes their body, mind, soul and unique personal dharma. As you explore who you are, remember that it is entirely up to you to cultivate gratitude for everything that you discover.

"No misfortune is so bad that whining about it won't make it worse."
~ Jeffrey R. Holland

DAY 18

Intention: I Am Compassionate

At Waking: Lemon Ginger Elixir & Herbal Tea

AM Walk: 21 minutes

AM Y/M: 42-minute AM Yoga & 21-minute AM Meditation

Breakfast: Smoothie 4: Pop-Eye

Lunch (12-2pm): Salad 4 & Vegetable Juice 4

Dinner (5-7pm): Steamed Brown Rice, Vegetable 4 & Soup 4

PM Walk: 21 minutes

PM Y/M: 21-minute PM Yoga & 42-minute PM Meditation

Treatment: Hot Epsom Salt Bath with Essential Oils

Mirror Theory: Write in your journal honest character descriptions of people who caught your attention today. How do you see yourself in these individuals?

Journal: How easy is it for you to forgive someone when they have crossed you? Explain the last instance when you were able to fully forgive someone who upset you. Are you able to understand their limitations and ignorance?

The power of compassion is a form of power that can and will change the world should we exercise it consciously, intentionally and often. Meaningful and heartfelt compassion properly expressed and utilized can and does transform lives and can quickly align consciousness with soul. The benefits of compassion are far reaching and extend far beyond those you may choose to assist, as well as yourself. In fact they impact the world and elevate the quality of consciousness on a Universal scale.

One of my favorite ways to deal with a particularly stressful day is with metta, or loving-kindness, practice. During metta, you will be acknowledging individuals in turn, accepting them as they are and sending thoughts for happiness and love their way. Metta can be a great healing step for difficult relationships and can strengthen your good relationships. It takes our egos out of the equation, thereby making it easier to heal ourselves and accept others.

During this period of unfolding your energies, you are slowly letting go of any defenses and/or protective mechanisms. You may feel raw, naked and vulnerable. This is normal. It is therefore utterly necessary to hold compassion for yourself at all times. Compassion for others will spring from the compassion you find for yourself once you realize and understand your personal limitations. Once you realize that we are all products of our upbringing, karmas and environment, it is easier to understand how our ignorance, quirks and patterning came to be.

Only when we learn to cultivate compassion will we be able to let go of self-defeating reactions such as judgments, fears, misperceptions and the like. Reacting to our judgments only sets us back onto the karmic treadmill, and the only way off this perpetuating cycle of comparing is through compassion. We do not always know or understand the circumstances that make people act the way that they do, and it oftentimes has nothing to do with us, but every time that you react, whether with excitement or anger, you are generating more karmas.

We are often our own worst critics, with voices of judgment and limiting beliefs holding negative chanting sessions in our minds. Allow yourself the space to err, to fall -- just as you would allow a child to fall when learning to walk. With continued patience and persistence, you will succeed.

Ask yourself who in your life that you harbor anger or judgment towards. Whether this person or group did something to offend you, or if you simply do not like how they act or behave -- even though you have not had direct experience with them (for example gang members). Throughout the day, can you think of this person or group without allowing emotions to surface or past events to overtake your mind? Try to understand why this person became who he or she became, and why he or she behaves as they do. Practice compassion by seeing their behaviors and actions in an unbiased light.

Practicing Metta

Begin your metta practice by finding a comfortable, relatively quiet spot in your home. Make sure there is nothing around you that could distract your thoughts –

188

like a television or project you've been meaning to work on. Sit in a comfortable position – cross-legged is recommended, or seated on a chair if you have knee issues. Calm your mind, close your eyes and bring your attention to the present moment. Breathe deeply.

Once you're feeling calm, offer yourself a prayer for your life. Say out loud:

> *May I be filled with loving-kindness*
> *May I be free of suffering*
> *May I be happy and at peace*

Now, think of someone in your life that you love. Pick someone who is easy to send positive thoughts towards -- your parents, spouse or best friend. Bring them to mind and visualize them happy, smiling. Keeping this person in mind, say out loud:

> *May you be filled with loving-kindness*
> *May you be free of suffering*
> *May you be happy and at peace*

Feel true happiness for their happiness. Take time to go through all the people in your life that you love -- your family members and friends, repeating the same process.

Now, think a "neutral" person. A person whom you do not have any feelings towards – for example, a stranger you saw on the street, your grocery store clerk, or a new co-worker. Repeat the same metta prayer for them.

Now, here will be the true test of your metta practice. Think of someone who is a difficult person in your life – an employer, a friend who betrayed you, someone who has hurt you. Bring them to mind and consider their lives. Try to imagine yourself in their lives and show compassion. When you're ready, say out loud:

> *May each of us be filled with loving-kindness*
>
> *May each of us be free of suffering*
>
> *May each of us be happy and at peace*

Take as much time as you need to practice metta with each group. When you're ready, consider everyone in your life; all of your loved ones, family, friends, co-workers, neighbors -- everyone you come in contact with throughout your days.

Lastly, go beyond the people in your life, consider all the people of the world, the people you've never met and will never meet. Say out loud:

May all beings be filled with loving-kindness

May all beings be free of suffering

May all beings be happy and at peace

Smile as you open your eyes and go about your day with loving kindness in your heart and mind.

Day 19

Intention: I Am Trusting

At Waking: Lemon Ginger Elixir & Herbal Tea

AM Walk: 21 minutes

AM Y/M: 42-minute AM Yoga & 21-minute AM Meditation

Breakfast: Smoothie 5: Water Pro

Lunch (12-2pm): Salad 5 & Vegetable Juice 5

Dinner (5-7pm): 1 cup steamed Brown Rice or Quinoa, Vegetable 5 & Soup 5

PM Walk: 21 minutes

PM Y/M: 21-minute PM Yoga & 42-minute Meditation

Treatment: 30-60 minute Gentle Thai Massage or Assisted Stretch

Mirror Theory: Write in your journal honest character descriptions of people who caught your attention today. How do you see yourself in these individuals?

Journal: Trusting in other people takes time and personal experience. Strengthen your trust in your dharma, a higher power and the karmic Laws of Nature. Write down times in your life when you were untrustworthy. Forgive yourself as you re-commit to living in accordance to Nature's laws with integrity.

As we focus on trust, in no way do I want to imply a blind trust, or to trust without seeing. In my yoga trainings I learned that the word trust emanated from the heart chakra, Anahata, which translates as "unstruck" – meaning unhurt, unbroken and whole.

Opening up the heart center is the key to healing and to trust. We must learn to forgive others and ourselves from past wrong doings. The past has no power in the present. It is over and done. Sometimes we confuse forgiveness with trust and respect. When we forgive we are not condoning the actions or behavior. We are simply forgiving it – we are letting go of trying to control it, and we are letting go of it controlling us.

This does not mean that we respect or trust any person who has wronged us. Respect and trust are ours to give. This is your power. Carrying a grievance does not punish the person who has wronged you; it only clutters your own heart.

Learning to Trust

Find encouraging friends. Good feelings are contagious. When we surround ourselves with positive people they usually have a positive effect on us. You may come to realize during this twenty-one day process that your friends aren't as positive as you thought. Maybe it is worth your time to investigate some new local groups with similar interests that you have. As you align with your dharma, observe if you resonate more harmoniously with different groups than you are currently in.

Communicate. Talking about what you are thinking and feeling to someone else, someone who is listening and who responds to what you say (not just reflecting back what you have said, but adding their own ideas and thoughts to the conversation) can help to shift old beliefs and programs. It can help your unconscious become conscious, unrecognized beliefs to be recognized, and your perspective to become clearer. Writing helps this process as well.

Practice. None of us learns to trust ourselves magically or instantaneously -- nor, should we. A perfect example is driving a car. We would not get into a car to drive for the first time -- even with all of the right instincts ready to go. Instead, we prepare and we practice. We take driver's education, then we get learner's permits, and we practice with experienced drivers until gradually we become mature, safe and trustworthy drivers. It is entirely acceptable and advised to take your time trusting others. Listen to your feelings.

Be trustworthy: If you want to trust yourself, be trustworthy with others. Try to give what you would like to receive, whether this is kindness, understanding, empathy, counsel, or simply a quiet presence. Try to recognize what your friends and family need from you and try to honestly give what you can, when you can, without sacrificing yourself. Setting boundaries is part of any caring relationship, and negotiating each other's needs helps you to know and trust yourself. It also helps others know and trust you as well.

DAY 20

Intention: I Am You

At Waking: Lemon Ginger Elixir & Herbal Tea

AM Walk: 21 minutes

AM Y/M: 42-minute AM Yoga & 21-minute AM Meditation

Breakfast: Smoothie 6: Mango Pro

Lunch (12-2pm): Salad 6 & Vegetable Juice 6

Dinner (5-7pm): 1 cup steamed Brown Rice or Quinoa, Vegetable 6 & Soup 6

PM Walk: 21 minutes

PM Y/M: 21-minute PM Yoga & 42-minute PM Meditation

Treatment: Coffee & Egg Facial

Mirror Theory: Write in your journal honest character descriptions of people who caught your attention today. How do you see yourself in these individuals?

Journal: Throughout the day, treat every person you come across as how you would like to be treated. At the end of the day, write down a complete recapitulation (abridged re-cap) of your day. As you review it, see yourself in each and every person that you encountered.

Aside from the fact that we are all one collective unconscious body, everyone in your life is your mirror. This is the greatest of all relationships secrets. What this means is that you are recognizing aspects of your own consciousness in another person -- giving you an opportunity to really see what you are focusing on, and ultimately, to grow. The qualities you most admire in others are your own and the same goes for those qualities you dislike. To change anything in your relationships, be the change you want to see.

The beauty of this understanding is that it leaves no room for blame, no room for judgment and no room to be a victim to another person's actions or words. There is only room for real love based on understanding, compassion and gratitude. Your relationships with others are your opportunity to experience yourself and grow. They are a perfect mirror of your inner relationship with yourself and the beliefs you have acquired about life and love. In order for you to recognize a certain quality in another, then it must be part of your conscious awareness. You could not see it otherwise.

Although The Dharma Zone guidelines minimize interactions with other people, positive and supportive relationships are the treasures of life. The time spent alone during the program should increase appreciation of your relationships when communication resumes. The space will also shed light on whether these relationships are trustworthy and true.

See Yourself In Others

All beings tremble before violence

All fear death

All love life

See Yourself In Others

Then whom can you hurt?

What harm can you do?

He who seeks happiness

By hurting those who seek happiness

Will never find happiness

For your brother is like you

He wants to be happy

Never harm him

You Too Will Find Happiness

In this life

And after you leave this life

~ Buddhist Teaching

DAY 21

Intention: I AM

At Waking: Lemon Ginger Elixir & Herbal Tea

AM Walk: 21 minutes

AM Y/M: 42-minute AM Yoga & 21-minute AM Meditation

Breakfast: Smoothie 7: Anti-Ox Pro

Lunch (12-2pm): Salad 7 & Vegetable Juice 7

Dinner (5-7pm): 1 cup steamed Brown Rice or Quinoa, Vegetable 7 & Soup 7

PM Walk: 21 minutes

PM Y/M: 21-minute PM Yoga & 42-minute PM Meditation

Treatment: Haircut and/or Professional Blow dry

Mirror Theory: Write in your journal honest character descriptions of people who caught your attention today. How do you see yourself in these individuals? How do you see yourself in these individuals?

Journal: Today is absolute self-appreciation day! It is truly magnificent when we look fondly into a mirror and appreciate what we see with genuine love. Write an appreciation letter to yourself. Ex: "Dear Self, I am so very proud of you that you stayed committed to your goals. You have improved your life so much from what it was before and you are committing to a healthier, more conscious lifestyle -- this is so admirable!"...

Congratulations! Today is a day to celebrate and to shine, exactly as you are. You should be very proud of yourself for having committed to the last twenty-one days. Look at what you have explored, realized and discovered. There is no end to this process -- this was merely the beginning. You have tasted your essence in a truer, less distracted state.

Achieving your goals is gratifying. The feeling of accomplishment makes the efforts worthwhile. This is a reason as to why we enjoy watching sporting events like football and basketball. We love a good game, and a good challenge, but mostly we love the stories of accomplishment. A gold medal is simply a pendant, unless the years of dedication, work, focus and commitment are added to its value.

Vision Board. A vision board is simply a visual representation or collage of the things that you want to have, be, or do in your life. It consists of a poster or foam board with pictures, drawings and/or writing arranged on it with these things that you want in your life -- or these things that you want to become. By selecting pictures and writing that charges you with feelings of commitment, you will continue to manifest these things into your life as you strengthen your focus on them.

Make a vision board that represents your twenty-one day Dharma Zone experiences. Let these images and words be reminders of who you are, what you love and believe. These will serve as a reminder for daily practice. It will also allow you to go deeper into the next twenty-one day Dharma Zone experience, when you choose to once again turn your awareness inward with a flashlight. Keep your board in a visible location in your work or home.

"Your time is limited, so don't waste it living someone else's life. Don't be trapped by dogma — which is living with the results of other people's thinking. Don't let the noise of others' opinions drown out your own inner voice. And most importantly, have the courage to follow your heart and intuition. They somehow already know what you truly want to become. Everything else is secondary." ~ *Steve Jobs*

Chapter 6: Preparing for The Dharma Zone

"He who is best prepared can best serve his moment of inspiration."
~ Samuel Taylor Coleridge

This chapter includes your daily meal recipes and treatment descriptions. If needed, you can alter the menus or treatments -- as long as you stay true to the guidelines of the program. Please consult with your doctor with any questions or areas of concern. Never over-exert yourself and discontinue the program if you feel weak or light-headed.

RECIPES

"The doctor of the future will no longer treat the human frame with drugs, but rather will cure and prevent disease with nutrition." ~ Thomas Edison

A. Elixirs & Tea:

Lemon Ginger Elixir (serves 1)

Ingredients:

- 1 small ripe lemon
- ½ raw peeled ginger
- honey or stevia

1. Boil water.

2. Juice the ginger and lemon.

3. Pour the ginger lemon juice into a hot mug or glass.

4. Add honey or stevia.

5. Add hot water, stir and drink when cooled.

Herbal Tea (serves 1)

Ingredients:

- 1 herbal tea bag
- honey or stevia

1. Boil water.

2. Place herbal tea bag in a hot mug.

3. Add hot water, sweeten to taste with honey or stevia.

B. Smoothies:

Smoothie 1: Blueberry Pro (serves 1)

Ingredients:

- ½ bag (oz) frozen organic blueberries
- 1 cup unsweetened almond or hemp milk
- 1 cup unsweetened coconut water
- 1 scoop royal jelly powder mix (YS Eco Bee Farms Royal Rush)
- 1 scoop greens powder (Vitaminerals Greens)
- 1 scoop vegan protein powder (Sunwarrior or similar)

Mix ingredients in a blender and serve.

Smoothie 2: Sweet Green (serves 1)

Ingredients:

- ½ banana
- 1 cup unsweetened coconut water
- 3 sprigs kale
- 1 scoop greens powder (Vitaminerals Greens)

Mix ingredients in a blender and serve.

Smoothie 3: Choco-co (serves 1)

Ingredients:

- 1 cup unsweetened almond or hemp milk
- 1 cup unsweetened coconut water
- 1 raw cacao powder
- 3 tbsp raw almond, cashew or peanut butter
- 1 tbsp fresh mint leaves

Mix ingredients in a blender and serve.

Smoothie 4: Pop-Eye (serves 1)

Ingredients:

- ½ cucumber
- 1 cup fresh squeezed orange juice
- 1 tbsp flax seed meal
- 1 oz wheatgrass juice (optional)

Mix ingredients in a blender and serve.

Smoothie 5: Water Pro (serves 1)

Ingredients:

- 1 cup unsweetened almond or hemp milk
- ½ banana
- 2 cups seedless watermelon
- ½ small lemon
- 1 scoop vegan protein powder (Sunwarrior or similar)

Mix ingredients in a blender and serve.

Smoothie 6: Royal Mango (serves 1)

Ingredients:

- 1 cup unsweetened almond or hemp milk
- ½ bag frozen mango pieces
- 1 scoop royal jelly powder mix (YS Eco Bee Farms Royal Rush)
- 1 scoop vegan protein powder (Sunwarrior or similar)

Mix ingredients in a blender and serve.

Smoothie 7: Berry Pro (serves 1)

Ingredients:

- 1 ½ cup unsweetened almond or hemp milk
- 1 cup organic frozen mixed berries
- 1 tbsp flax seed meal
- 1 scoop greens powder (Vitaminerals Greens)
- 1 scoop vegan protein powder (Sunwarrior or similar)

Mix ingredients in a blender and serve.

C. Salads:

Salad 1: Spring Blend (serves 1)

Ingredients:

- 3 cups spring mix lettuce
- 2 small ripe tomatoes, sliced
- 1 ripe avocado, sliced

Dressing:

- 3 tbsp extra virgin olive oil
- 1½ tbsp Braggs Liquid Aminos

Mix ingredients in a large bowl. Add dressing to taste.

Salad 2: Vegan "Caesar" (serves 4)

Ingredients:

- 3 cups chopped romaine leaves

Dressing:

- 1 ripe avocado
- 3 tsp lemon juice
- 2 tsp water
- 3 cloves of garlic, minced
- 1 tsp caper brine
- 1 tbsp capers
- 2 tbsp Dijon mustard
- Sea salt and fresh ground pepper, to taste
- ¼ cup hemp seeds

Blend the avocado, lemon juice, water, garlic, brine, capers, mustard salt and pepper in your food processor or blender until smooth. If it needs some thinning out (depending on the size of your avocado) you can add a touch

more water. The end result will be the consistency of pudding. Keep it this way to maintain ultra creaminess.
Spoon dressing into a bowl and stir in hemp seeds.

Place romaine in a large salad bowl, drop dressing on top and rotate leaves until coated to preference.

Salad 3: Spinach Papaya (serves 1)

Ingredients:

- 3 cups Spinach
- ½ fresh papaya, diced
- 4 tsp raw pine nuts
- 1 ripe avocado, sliced

Dressing:

- 3 tbsp extra virgin olive oil
- 1½ tbsp Braggs Liquid Aminos

Mix ingredients in a large bowl. Add dressing to taste.

Salad 4: Cucumber Tomato Salad (serves 1)

Ingredients:

- ½ large cucumber, sliced
- 1 medium tomato, cubed
- ¼ small red onion, chopped
- ½ handful fresh basil, chopped
- garlic salt and pepper, to taste

Dressing:

- 2 tbsp balsamic or apple cider vinegar
- 3 tbsp extra virgin olive oil

Mix ingredients in a large bowl. Add dressing to taste.

Salad 5: Butternut Kale (serves 4)

Ingredients:

- 1 small butternut squash, peeled, seeded, and cut into 1-inch cubes
- 3 tbsp extra virgin olive oil
- salt and pepper, to taste
- 1 small bunch kale in bite-sized pieces (remove any tough stems)
- 3 tbsp sliced organic almonds (optional)

Dressing:

- 1/3 c. tahini
- 1/3 c. water
- 2 tbsp fresh lemon juice

Preheat oven to 425 degrees. Line a rimmed baking sheet with parchment paper for baking.

In a large bowl, toss butternut squash with 1 tablespoon of olive oil, salt and pepper. Transfer to baking sheet and roast about 30 minutes, stirring halfway through cooking time.
While squash is baking, place kale in large bowl. Drizzle with one tablespoon of olive oil and season with salt and pepper. Using your hands, massage kale leaves until it softens and wilts, about 3-5 minutes. (Kale will taste mild when it's done.) Set aside.

Whisk together tahini, water, lemon juice, and remaining tablespoon of olive oil. Add salt and pepper to taste.

Mix the kale and butternut squash and tahini dressing in a large bowl. Serve.

Salad 6: Greek Chickpea Salad (serves 4)

Ingredients:

- 1 (15 ounce) cans garbanzo beans, drained
- 2 cucumbers, halved lengthwise and sliced
- 6 cherry tomatoes, halved
- ¼ red onion, chopped
- 1 clove garlic, minced
- ½ (15 ounce) can black olives, drained and chopped

Dressing:

- ½ cup vegan Italian-style salad dressing
- ½ lemon, juiced
- ½ tsp garlic salt
- ½ tsp ground black pepper

Combine the beans, cucumbers, tomatoes, red onion, garlic, olives, cheese, salad dressing, lemon juice, garlic salt and pepper. Toss together and refrigerate 2 hours before serving. Serve chilled.

Salad 7: Quinoa Avocado Salad (serves 4)

Ingredients:

- ¾ cups quinoa, rinsed very well
- 1 ¼ cups water
- ½ clove garlic, minced or pressed
- ¼ tsp sea or pink Himalayan salt (optional)
- ½ large cucumber, peeled, seeded, and diced
- 1 medium-large tomatoes, finely chopped
  kernels of 1 ears of cooked corn (about ½ cup)
- ¾ cups cooked chickpeas
- ¼ cup scallions, thinly sliced
- ½ cup parsley — minced
- ¼ cup fresh mint — minced
- 1 ripe avocado, peeled, pitted, and diced (reserve a few slices for garnish)

224

Dressing:

- ¼ cup freshly squeezed lime juice (NOT lemon)
- ½ tbsp vegetable broth
- ½ tsp salt, or to taste (optional)
- 1 dash of ground pepper
- ½ clove garlic, pressed or minced
- ¼ tsp chipotle chili pepper

To cook the quinoa in a pressure cooker, place it and the water, garlic, and salt in the cooker and lock the lid. Over high heat, bring to high pressure and cook for one minute. Remove from heat and allow the pressure to come down naturally. Fluff the quinoa and allow it to cool. (To cook it on the stove, use 3 cups of water. Bring to a boil, add the quinoa, cover tightly, reduce heat, and cook until all water is absorbed, about 15 minutes. Fluff and cool.)

Combine all of the vegetables in a large bowl. Add the quinoa and mix well.

Whisk the dressing ingredients together and pour over the salad. Mix well.

Garnish with avocado slices and serve.

D. Fresh Squeezed Juices

Juice 1: Rise and Shine (serves 1)

Ingredients:

- 1 granny smith apple
- 1 Fuji apple
- 2 cucumbers
- 6 celery stalks
- 1" piece of ginger
- 1 dash of cinnamon
- 2 tbsp apple cider vinegar

Juice the apples, cucumber, celery and ginger. Stir or blend in cinnamon and apple cider vinegar.

Juice 2: V Great (serves 1)

Ingredients:

- 2 red or Fuji apples
- 1 beet
- 2 carrots
- ½ cucumber
- 2 celery stalks
- 2 cups of spinach
- 2 parsley sprigs
- 1 dash of cayenne pepper
- 1 dash of Himalayan pink salt OR sea salt

Juice the apples, beet, carrots, cucumber, celery, spinach and parsley. Stir or blend in cayenne pepper and salt.

Juice 3: Power Green Juice (serves 1)

Ingredients:

- 2 granny smith apples
- 2 carrots
- 2 celery stalks
- 1 lemon
- 1" piece of ginger
- 1" piece of turmeric
- 1 scoop greens powder (Vitaminerals Greens)

Juice the apples, carrots, celery, lemon, ginger and turmeric. Stir or blend in Vitaminerals Greens (or your favorite vegan greens blend).

Juice 4: Sweet Goodness (serves 1)

Ingredients:

- 1 cup seedless red grapes
- 2 fuji apples
- 2 carrots
- 2 celery stalks
- 4 kale stalks
- 2 cups of spinach

Juice the grapes, apples, celery, kale and spinach.

Juice 5: Earth Magic (serves 1)

Ingredients:

- ½ fennel bulb
- ½ romaine lettuce head
- 2 celery stalks
- 4 kale stalks
- ½ lemon
- 1" piece of ginger

- 1" piece of turmeric
- 1 scoop greens powder (Vitaminerals Greens)

Juice the fennel, romaine, celery, kale, lemon, ginger and turmeric. Stir or blend in Vitaminerals Greens (or your favorite vegan greens blend).

Juice 6: Cool Veg (serves 1)

Ingredients:

- 3 celery stalks
- 4 kale stalks
- 2 cups of spinach
- 2 cucumbers
- 1 granny smith apple
- 3 sprigs of parsley
- 1" piece of ginger
- 1" piece of turmeric
- 2 tbsp apple cider vinegar

Juice the celery, kale, spinach, cucumbers, apple, parsley ginger and turmeric. Stir in the apple cider vinegar.

Juice 7: Red Cab (serves 1)

Ingredients:

- 1 cup red cabbage
- 2 cups red seedless grapes
- 2 red or fuji apples

Juice the red cabbage, grapes and apples.

E. Soups

Soup 1: Vegetable Soup with Avocado (serves 1)

Ingredients:

- ¼ sliced onion
- 1 garlic clove
- 1 sliced celery stalk
- 1 sliced large carrot
- ½ cup broccoli
- ½ cup cauliflower
- 3 cups vegetable broth
- 1 avocado

Bring vegetable broth to a boil. Add onion, garlic, celery, carrot, broccoli and cauliflower to the broth. Boil for 3 minutes, then let simmer until cauliflower and carrots are tender. Serve hot with avocado on top.

Soup 2: Hearty Miso Soup (serves 2)

Ingredients:

- 5 dried shiitake mushrooms
- 2 to 3 tablespoons white, gluten-free miso paste or powder
- ½ cup tubed silken or firm tofu (optional)
- 2 cups spinach or watercress
- ¼ cup wakame seaweed or shredded nori
- ¼ cup shredded carrots
- 1 tbsp thinly sliced scallions

Directions:

Pour 2 cups of boiling water over the dried shiitakes and allow them to soak for 30 minutes.
Meanwhile, boil 4 cups of water for about 30 minutes.
Remove the mushrooms from their soaking liquid, reserving the liquid.
Discarding the stems, thinly slice the shiitakes, and add to boiling water.

Make sure to hold back the gritty mushroom sediment that collects at the bottom.

Stir in the miso paste to taste and tofu, spinach, wakame, carrots and scallions. Bring the soup to just under a boil (boiling will kill the healthy, probiotic bacteria in the miso). Serve.

Soup 3: Curried Lentil Soup (serves 2)

Ingredients:

- ½ large clove garlic
- 1 piece (¼ inch long) peeled fresh ginger
- ½ small bulb fennel, cored and cut into large chunks (or ½ small celery stalk, cut into large chunks)
- ½ small carrot, peeled and cut into large chunks
- ½ small parsnip, peeled and cut into large chunks
- ½ large shallot, cut in half
- 1 ½ tbsp raw coconut oil
- 1 tsp curry powder
- ½ cup brown lentils, picked over and rinsed
- ½ qt. homemade or low salt vegetable broth
- pinch of sea salt
- pinch of freshly ground black pepper

Pulse the garlic and ginger in a food processor until chopped. Add the fennel or celery, carrot, parsnip, and shallot. Pulse until coarsely chopped.

Melt the coconut oil in a 4-qt. saucepan over medium-high heat. Add the chopped vegetables and cook, stirring, until softened, about 3 minutes. Add the curry powder and cook, stirring, until the curry powder is fragrant (about 30 seconds). Add the lentils, broth, salt, and pepper. Bring the soup to a boil over high heat, reduce the heat to maintain a brisk simmer, cover, and cook until the lentils are tender, 25 to 30 minutes.

Transfer 1 cup of the soup to a blender or a food processor and purée until smooth. Stir the purée back into the soup along with the remaining coconut oil. Season to taste with salt and pepper, and adjust the consistency with water, to preference.

Soup 4: Carrot Ginger (serves 2)

Ingredients:

- 3 tbsp extra virgin olive oil
- ½ yellow onion, diced
- ¼ cup fresh ginger, minced
- 4 cups chopped and peeled carrots (about 1½ pounds)
- 3 cups vegetable broth
- 1½ cups orange juice
- 1 dash nutmeg
- salt and pepper to taste

In a large pot, sauté onions and ginger in olive oil until soft, about 3-5 minutes.

Add carrots and vegetable broth. Reduce heat to medium. Allow to simmer for about 40 minutes, or until carrots are soft.

Add orange juice and stir well.
Using a food processor or blender, process soup until smooth.
Return to pot or serving bowl and add nutmeg, salt and pepper, stirring well.
Serve.

Soup 5: Garbanzo Bean & Kale Soup (serves 3)

Ingredients:

- 2 tbsp extra virgin olive oil
- 5 cloves Garlic, Minced
- 32 ounces vegetable soup broth
- 1 pound kale, rinsed
- ½ whole large zucchini, quartered
- ½ cups baby portabella mushrooms
- ½ whole onion, diced
- 1 can (15 ounces) garbanzo beans, drained and rinsed
- 1 dash salt and pepper, to taste
- 1 tsp nutmeg

In a large pot, add 1 tbsp of olive oil and 3 cloves of garlic over medium heat. Sauté until garlic is lightly browned. Add 1 cup vegetable stock and kale to pot. Stir to ensure kale is coated with the garlic/broth mixture. Cook kale on medium-high for 5 minutes covered, and then 5 minutes longer, uncovered, until wilted. Add salt and pepper to taste.

While kale is cooking, in a separate pan over medium heat, sauté remaining olive oil, remaining garlic, zucchini, mushrooms, and onion until tender (3-5 minutes.)

Once kale is cooked, add zucchini, mushroom, and onion mixture to the large pot with the kale. Add garbanzo beans, remaining vegetable stock and nutmeg. Cook on medium heat for 10 minutes, until the flavors have married and the garbanzo beans are soft but not mushy. Add salt and pepper if necessary. Serve.

Soup 6: Cabbage Vegetable Soup (serves 2)

Ingredients:

- 1 medium leek (white and light green parts only)
- 1 tbsp extra virgin olive oil
- ½ medium yellow onion, diced small
- 1 medium carrot, diced small
- 1 celery stalks, diced small
- 1 garlic cloves, minced
- ¼ medium Yukon Gold potato, peeled and diced small
- 3 cups low-sodium vegetable broth
- 1 bay leaf
- ¼ head green cabbage, cored and thinly sliced
- Sea salt and ground pepper, to taste
- 1 tsp apple cider vinegar
- ½ tbsp chopped fresh thyme leaves

Halve the leeks lengthwise. Rinse thoroughly, pat dry, and cut into 1/2-inch slices. In a large heavy pot, heat oil over medium-high. Add onion, carrots, and celery. Cook, stirring occasionally, until softened (about 5 minutes). Add leeks and garlic and cook, stirring, until leeks begin to soften (2 minutes).

234

Add potato, broth, and bay leaves and bring to a boil. Stir in cabbage and season generously with salt and pepper.

Return soup to a boil, then reduce to a simmer. Cover and cook until vegetables are tender (15 to 20 minutes). Remove from heat; stir in vinegar and thyme. Season with salt and pepper.

Soup 7: Broccoli Puree Soup

Ingredients:

- ½ large onion, chopped
- 1 large garlic clove, chopped
- 1 tbsp extra virgin olive oil
- 1 pinch black pepper
- 1 pinch dried Thyme
- ½ bunch of broccoli (cleaned, stems removed and broken into smaller florets)
- ½ head of Cauliflower, cleaned and cut into large pieces
- 2 cups vegetable broth
- 1 avocado

Heat a large soup pot with a splash of olive oil, onion, garlic and spices over medium high heat. When it starts to sizzle reduce heat to medium and cook about 5 minutes until lightly brown, softened and fragrant, stirring occasionally.

Add the cauliflower and broccoli and cook these a few minutes with the onions. Add the hot broth to the soup pot, increase the heat back to medium high and bring to a boil. Reduce heat back to medium, partially cover and simmer for about 30 minutes until the vegetables are very soft and you can mash them with a fork.

Remove soup from the stovetop and let it cool a bit. Purée the contents with a blender or food processor until smooth. Add more broth depending upon how thick you want your soup. Garnish with the avocado on top.

F. Vegetable Sides

Vegetable Side 1: Spinach & Edamame (serves 1)

Ingredients:

- 1 cup spinach
- 1 cup shelled edamame
- 1 tsp raw coconut oil or extra virgin olive oil

Fill a large saucepan with about an inch of water, and insert a steamer basket. Bring the water to a boil, and add the broccoli into the basket. Reduce the heat to a simmer and cover, allowing the broccoli to steam for 6-8 minutes, or until fork tender.

In a separate saucepan, boil the shelled edamame beans in water.

Combine the spinach and edamame in a bowl when complete. Stir in coconut or extra virgin olive oil. Serve.

Vegetable Side 2: Cauliflower Mash (serves 2)

Ingredients:

- Medium-sized head of cauliflower, chopped into florets (about 1½ lbs)
- 3 roasted garlic cloves
- 1 tsp fresh thyme leaves
- 1 tsp fresh chives, chopped
- salt and pepper, to taste

Fill a large saucepan with about an inch of water, and insert a steamer basket. Bring the water to a boil, and add the cauliflower florets. Reduce the heat to a simmer and cover, allowing the cauliflower to steam for 6-8 minutes, or until fork tender.

Drain the steamed cauliflower, and transfer to a blender or food processor. Add in the roasted garlic cloves and seasonings. Process the mixture to your desired texture.

Feel free to add any additional liquid for blending -- a splash of almond milk or water, if needed.

Vegetable Side 3: Carrots & Snow Peas (serves 1)

Ingredients:

- 1 cup carrots, sliced
- 1 cup snow pea pods or green beans
- ½ lemon

Fill a large saucepan with about an inch of water, and insert a steamer basket. Bring the water to a boil, and add the carrots. Reduce the heat to a simmer and cover, allowing the broccoli to steam for 3-5 minutes, or until fork tender.

Add the snow pea pods or green beans with the carrots. Steam an additional 2-4 minutes.

Squeeze ½ lemon on top. Serve.

Vegetable Side 4: Pepper & Onion Stir-Fry (serves 1)

Ingredients:

- ½ cup red bell pepper, sliced
- ½ cup yellow bell pepper, sliced
- ½ cup green bell pepper, sliced
- ¼ medium sized onion, sliced
- 1 pinch sea salt
- 1 pinch black pepper
- 1 tsp raw coconut oil or extra virgin olive oil

Wash and halve the peppers (remove seeds and ribs). Cut into 1/4-inch thick slices.

Heat oil in a large skillet. Add peppers and onions. Sauté over medium-high heat for 5 to 8 minutes. Stir constantly or until golden brown and tender. Sprinkle with salt and pepper, to taste.

Vegetable Side 5: Steamed Broccoli (serves 1)

Ingredients:

- 1 cup broccoli florets
- 1 tsp raw coconut oil or extra virgin olive oil

Fill a large saucepan with about an inch of water, and insert a steamer basket. Bring the water to a boil, and add the broccoli florets. Reduce the heat to a simmer and cover, allowing the broccoli to steam for 5-7 minutes, or until fork tender.

Stir in coconut or extra virgin olive oil. Serve.

Vegetable Side 6: Sweet Potato Mash (serves 2)

Ingredients:

- 1 or 2 large sweet potatoes or yams, chopped
- ¼ ounce can of coconut milk
- 1 pinch of ginger
- 1 pinch of curry
- 1 tbsp extra virgin olive oil
- salt and pepper, to taste

In a large pot, cover the yams or sweet potatoes with water and bring to a boil. Allow to simmer for at least 15 minutes, or until soft.

Remove the skin of the sweet potatoes and mash to desired consistency.

Add remaining ingredients. Mix well. Serve.

Vegetable Side 7: Steamed Red Cabbage

Ingredients:

- 1 cup red cabbage
- ½ lemon

Fill a large saucepan with about an inch of water, and insert a steamer basket. Bring the water to a boil, and add the red cabbage. Reduce the heat to a simmer and cover, allowing the cabbage to steam for 6-8 minutes, or until fork tender.

Squeeze ½ lemon on top. Serve.

G. Steamed Brown Rice or Quinoa

Ingredients:

- 1 cup brown rice or quinoa
- 1½ cup water
- 1 pinch of salt
- 1 tbsp raw coconut oil.

Pressure Cooker:
Place the rice or quinoa with the water and salt in the cooker and lock the lid. Over high heat, bring to high pressure and cook for one minute. Remove from heat and allow the pressure to come down naturally. Fluff and allow to cool.

Stovetop:
Bring water to a boil. Add the rice or quinoa and cover tightly. Reduce heat, and cook until all water is absorbed (about 15 minutes). Fluff and allow to cool.

Stir the coconut oil into the rice or quinoa.

TREATMENTS

"Do something every day that is loving toward your body and gives you the opportunity to enjoy the sensations of your body." ~ *Golda Poretsky*

Day 1: Epsom Salt Bath with Essential Oils

Ingredients:

- 3-4 cups Epsom salts
- 5-10 drops of essential oils (optional)

Application:

1. Fill the bathtub with hot or warm water. Add about three to four cups of Epsom salts to the water. Swirl the water with your hands and allow the Epsom salts to dissolve.

2. Enhance your Epsom salt bath with five to ten drops of your favorite essential oils. Add lavender, rose or chamomile essential oil to relieve stress. Add the essential oils just before you step into the tub, as essential oils evaporate quickly in warm water.

3. Relax and soak in the Epsom salt bath for ten to fifteen minutes.

4. Take a warm shower to rinse the Epsom salts from your skin.

5. Apply moisturizer.

Day 2: Dry Brush & Salt Scrub

Ingredients:

- 1 cup Epsom salts
- ½ cup oil of choice (virgin coconut, castor oil, sesame oil, almond oil or jojoba oil)
- Create your own items (lemons, oranges, cucumbers, ginger, camphor, honey)
- 5 drops of essential oils of choice (rose, lavender, tea tree)
- Dry Brush

Application:

1. Mix the Epsom salts, and coconut oil in a bowl with a spoon. Add any essential oils.

2. Dry brush your entire body with a dry body brush. Start with your right leg, moving lymph and blood towards your heart – then switch to your left leg and arms.

3. Step into a bathtub. Put on loofah mitts or exfoliating gloves. If you do not have a bath mitt, don't worry; you can use your hands.

4. Take a spoonful of the mixture into your palms or your gloves and then rub the mixture all over your body in a circular motion. For tougher areas such as the knees, soles and elbows, spend extra scrubbing time. On places like the chest, neck, and stomach, where the skin is thinner, take it easy with the scrubbing and instead use cleanser on a washcloth to exfoliate. If you feel the salt is too harsh on your skin, rinse off the bath mitts and then spoon only the oil onto the mitts to continue.

5. Once your entire body is scrubbed well, rinse thoroughly.

6. Pat your skin dry. The salt will have exfoliated your skin nicely with the help of the loofah and the oil should leave skin soft and moisturized. You shouldn't even need to follow the bath with a moisturizer, but it never hurts to add more moisturizer.

7. **Please be careful** – the oil in this scrub can build up on your bathtub. Make sure to clean this after your scrub so the next person who gets in your bath doe not slip.

Day 3: Facial Mask - Apple Cider Vinegar & Clay

Ingredients:

- 2 tsp kaolin or green clay
- 1½ tbsp aloe vera gel
- 1 tbsp jojoba oil

- 1 tbsp unpasteurized apple cider vinegar
- 2 drops essential oil of choice (rose, lavender or tea tree)

Application:

1. Apply the jojoba oil to your clean face.

2. Mix clay together with the aloe vera gel, apple cider vinegar and essential oils.

3. Apply the mix on top of your oiled skin.

4. Allow the clay mix to dry (10-15 minutes).

5. Rinse and cleanse and follow with a thin layer of moisturizer.

Day 4: Colon Cleanse

Ingredients:

- 1 disposable Fleet enema OR
- 1 disposable Fleet suppository OR
- 1 herbal laxative tea bag

Application:

1. Wash your hands thoroughly.

2. Moisten your anus with virgin coconut oil.

3. Lie on your side with your lower leg straightened out and your upper leg bent forward toward your stomach.
4. Insert the suppository or enema tip, pointed end first, with your finger until it passes the muscular sphincter of the rectum. If using an enema, squeeze the saline solution or water into your rectum.

5. Remain lying down for about 5 minutes to avoid having the suppository or solution come out.

6. Discard used materials and wash your hands thoroughly.

7. Be prepared to have a full bowel movement.

NOTE: If you are accustomed to enemas or high irrigation colonics, you can use a home enema bag with purified water or schedule a colonic with a respected, certified colon hydro-therapist.
If you are not comfortable with any of the colon cleanse options, drinking herbal laxative tea is a wonderful alternative.

Day 5: Gargle with 3% Hydrogen Peroxide

Ingredients:

- 3% Hydrogen Peroxide (from drugstore)

Application:

1. Put three ounces of hydrogen peroxide into a cup.

2. Dilute the hydrogen peroxide with three ounces of warm water.

3. Pour the mixture into your mouth, but do not swallow.

4. Swish the liquid around in between your teeth. This will kill bacteria on the gums.

5. Gargle the liquid by tilting your head back, opening your mouth and exhaling out of your throat. This will help to kill the bacteria that cause sore throats. ***Do not swallow.**

6. Prevent swallowing by closing your mouth and continuing to exhale out of your throat as you lower your head over a sink.

7. Spit all of the liquid into the sink.

8. Rinse with water and follow with brushing and flossing.

Day 6: Foot Scrub & Bath (optional Pedicure)

Ingredients:

- 2 cups Epsom or Sea salts
- ½ cup sesame or almond oil
- 10 drops essential oils of choice (lavender, tea tree, lemon, rose)
- ½ gallon of milk
- 1 bag of marbles (optional)

Application:

1. Prepare your salt foot scrub by combining two cups of salts and 1/2 cup of oil in a plastic bowl. Add ten drops of essential oils of choice and stir thoroughly with a spoon.

2. Pour 1/2 gallon of whole milk into a large saucepan. Heat on the lowest setting for about fifteen minutes, stirring occasionally. After about fifteen minutes, pour the milk into a tub that is large enough for both feet.

3. For an extra sensory exercise, add a bag of marbles to the milk bath and sink your feet into your healing foot spa. Play with the marbles with your toes, massaging your feet. Soak for fifteen or twenty minutes.

4. Remove one foot from the tub and pat dry. Apply a bit of your salt foot scrub to your feet and massage into calluses or dry spots, around the nails and between the toes. Scrub directly over the tub so that excess salt can fall into the tub. When ready, switch feet. When finished scrubbing both feet, dip both feet into the milk bath to remove the salt scrub.

5. Pat your feet dry and take this opportunity to trim your toenails, push back cuticles. Scrape away calluses. Finish by applying a heavy foot cream and covering your feet with thick socks.

Day 7: Body Massage (optional Sauna)

Massage

The benefits of massage demonstrate that it is an effective treatment for reducing stress, pain and muscle tension.

Beyond the benefits for specific conditions or diseases, some people enjoy massage because it often involves caring, comfort, and a sense of relaxation.

Sauna

Saunas are known to improve overall health and are used to treat a number of ailments. The heat from a sauna raises body temperature, which causes blood vessels to dilate and increase circulation. When blood flow is increased it accelerates the natural healing process of your body.

The heat from a sauna causes you to sweat. Increased circulation helps to cleanse your skin from the inside out, giving you a healthy glow. Increased circulation improves skin tone and elasticity, which decreases the visibility of lines and wrinkles. Sweating flushes toxins and bacteria from your epidermal layer, sweat ducts and pores. This gives your skin a clearer and softer appearance.

Everyday stress can have an effect on your health. Saunas provide relief from stress in a number of ways. The heat from a sauna naturally relaxes your body. This relieves muscle tension and creates a calming effect. The heat also stimulates the release of endorphins in your body. Endorphins are chemicals in your body that create a peaceful, euphoric feeling and naturally relieve pain.

250

Since the skin is our largest organ, it plays an important role in eliminating undesirable toxins. Some physicians refer to the skin as a third kidney.

An infrared sauna is slightly different than a normal sauna. It makes the same rays that come from the sun, filtering out the UV radiation, giving you only the infrared radiation. This infrared penetrates into your skin and surface muscle tissue, which can be beneficial in reducing muscle spasms, joint stiffness and achiness.

*WARNING: Consult with your doctor before using a sauna. Limit time to ten-minute sessions. Drink a lot of water.

Inquire in your local area of a respected, certified massage therapist to schedule a Swedish or Deep Tissue massage. It is recommended to enjoy a sauna prior to your massage, if this is possible and permitted by your doctor.

Day 8: Hot Oil / Coconut Milk Hair Treatment

Ingredients:

- 1 can unsweetened coconut milk
- 2 tbsp virgin coconut oil

Application:

1. **The night before your treatment,** pour a can of unsweetened coconut milk in a bowl and refrigerate overnight so it hardens.

2. Warm the coconut oil. Massage to scalp and hair.

3. Apply the hardened milk from roots to ends over the coconut oil.

4. Comb the mixture through your hair.

5. Leave on for 15 to 20 minutes.

6. Shampoo, rinse and comb out.

If you have dry ends but your scalp tends to get oily, apply this mask only to the bottom half of hair, keeping it away from your scalp.

Day 9: Epsom Salt Bath with Essential Oils

Ingredients:

- 3-4 cups Epsom salts
- 5-10 drops of essential oils (optional)

Application:

1. Fill the bathtub with hot or warm water. Add about three to four cups of Epsom salts to the water. Swirl the water with your hands and allow the Epsom salts to dissolve.

2. Enhance your Epsom salt bath with five to ten drops of your favorite essential oils. Add lavender, rose or chamomile essential oil to relieve stress. Add the essential oils just before you step into the tub, as essential oils evaporate quickly in warm water.

3. Relax and soak in the Epsom salt bath for ten to fifteen minutes.

4. Take a warm shower to rinse the Epsom salts from your skin.

5. Apply moisturizer.

Day 10: Hydrogen Peroxide Bath

Ingredients:

- 1 cup 35% Food Grade Hydrogen Peroxide (*see warning below) OR 6 bottles of 3% Hydrogen Peroxide (from a drugstore)

*WARNING 1: 35% Food Grade Hydrogen Peroxide will burn your skin undiluted.

*WARNING 2: Do not put your hair in the water as it could bleach your color slightly.

Application:

1. Fill the bathtub with hot or warm water. Add one cup of 35% Food Grade Hydrogen Peroxide or 6 bottles of 3% Hydrogen Peroxide to the water.

2. Relax and soak in the oxygenating Hydrogen Peroxide bath for ten to fifteen minutes.

3. Apply moisturizer.

Day 11: Baking Soda Bath with Essential Oils

Ingredients:

- 1 lb box of Baking Soda
- 5-10 drops of essential oils (optional)

Application:

1. Fill the bathtub with hot or warm water. Add 1 cup of Baking Soda to the water. Swirl the water with your hands and allow the Baking Soda to dissolve.

2. Enhance your bath with five to ten drops of your favorite essential oils. Add lavender, rose or chamomile essential oil to relieve stress. Add the essential oils just before you step into the tub, as essential oils evaporate quickly in warm water.

3. Relax and soak in the bath for ten to fifteen minutes. Baking Soda neutralized acidity. This will leave your skin feeling smooth and clean.

4. Pat dry and apply moisturizer.

Day 12: Lemon & Honey Facial

Ingredients:

- 1 ripe lemon
- 3 tbsp honey

Application:

1. Carefully cut the lemon into quarters.

2. Rub the lemon meat, juice and rind onto your cleansed skin.

3. Apply the honey, massaging over the lemon.

4. Massage for 5-10 minutes.

5. Rinse and cleanse.

6. Follow with a thin layer of moisturizer.

Day 13: Dry Brush & Sugar Scrub

Ingredients:

- 1 cup brown sugar
- ¼ cup oil virgin coconut oil
- 3 tbsp honey
- 5 drops of essential oils of choice (rose, lavender, tea tree)
- Dry Brush

Application:

1. Mix the brown sugar, coconut oil and honey in a bowl with a spoon. Add essential oils.

2. Dry brush your entire body with a dry body brush. Start with your right leg, moving lymph and blood towards your heart – then switch to your left leg and arms.

3. Step into a bathtub. Put on loofah mitts or exfoliating gloves. If you do not have a bath mitt, don't worry; you can use your hands.

4. Take a spoonful of the mixture into your palms or your gloves and then rub the mixture all over your body in a circular motion. For tougher areas such as the knees, soles and elbows, spend extra scrubbing time. On places like the chest, neck, and stomach, where the skin is thinner, take it easy with the scrubbing and instead use cleanser on a washcloth to exfoliate. If you feel the sugar is too harsh on your skin, rinse off the bath mitts and then spoon only the oil onto the mitts to continue.

5. Once your entire body is scrubbed well, rinse thoroughly.

6. Pat your skin dry. The sugar will have exfoliated your skin nicely with the help of the loofah and the oil and honey should leave skin soft and moisturized. You shouldn't even need to follow the bath with a moisturizer, but it never hurts to add more moisturizer.

Please be careful – the oil in this scrub can build up on your bathtub. Make sure to clean this after your scrub so the next person who gets in your bath doe not slip.

Day 14: Foot Reflexology

Reflexologists believe that different areas on your feet and hands correspond to other parts of your body, and massaging them stimulates your parasympathetic nervous system to heal itself.

For 3,000 years Chinese practitioners have used reflexology to re-balance qi (the life force flowing through energy channels) to treat a number of conditions. It can work alongside conventional Western medical medicine to promote healing and improve wellbeing and vitality.

Inquire in your local area of a respected, certified spa or clinic offering reflexology treatments. If it is too difficult to find a reflexology treatment, please repeat the Foot Scrub & Bath from Day 6.

Day 15: Acupuncture Treatment

Oriental medicine is a holistic approach to health, which is based on the treatment of all bodily systems. Acupuncture benefits the improvement of physical health conditions and it instills a feeling of increased mental clarity.

Acupuncture works directly with the body's energy or qi, as acupuncture practitioners believe that all illnesses are a result of the natural flow of energy through the body becoming stuck, depleted or weakened -- thus making the individual susceptible to illness. Acupuncture benefits the rebalance of qi through treatment of specific acupoints related to symptoms or illness present. Treatment is effective in removing these energy obstructions.

Inquire in your local area of a respected, certified acupuncture clinic. You do not have to have an "ailment" to receive acupuncture. Take note of the increased energy and circulation post treatment.

Day 16: Body Massage (optional Sauna)

Massage

The benefits of massage demonstrate that it is an effective treatment for reducing stress, pain and muscle tension.

Beyond the benefits for specific conditions or diseases, some people enjoy massage because it often involves caring, comfort, and a sense of relaxation.

Sauna

Saunas are known to improve overall health and are used to treat a number of ailments. The heat from a sauna raises body temperature, which causes blood vessels to dilate and increase circulation. When blood flow is increased it accelerates the natural healing process of your body.

The heat from a sauna causes you to sweat. Increased circulation helps to cleanse your skin from the inside out, giving you a healthy glow. Increased circulation improves skin tone and elasticity, which decreases the visibility of lines and wrinkles. Sweating flushes toxins and bacteria from your epidermal layer, sweat ducts and pores. This gives your skin a clearer and softer appearance.

Everyday stress can have an effect on your health. Saunas provide relief from stress in a number of ways. The heat from a sauna naturally relaxes your body. This relieves muscle tension and creates a calming effect. The heat also stimulates the release of endorphins in your body. Endorphins are chemicals in your body that create a peaceful, euphoric feeling and naturally relieve pain.

Since the skin is our largest organ, it plays an important role in eliminating undesirable toxins. Some physicians refer to the skin as a third kidney.

An infrared sauna is slightly different than a normal sauna. It makes the same rays that come from the sun, filtering out the UV radiation, giving you only the infrared radiation. This infrared penetrates into your skin and surface muscle tissue, which can be beneficial in reducing muscle spasms, joint stiffness and achiness.

*WARNING: Consult with your doctor before using a sauna. Limit time to ten-minute sessions. Drink a lot of water.

Inquire in your local area of a respected, certified massage therapist to schedule a Swedish or Deep Tissue massage. It is recommended to enjoy a sauna prior to your massage, if this is possible and permitted by your doctor.

Day 17: Coffee Body Scrub

Ingredients:

- 1 cup Epsom salts
- ½ cup virgin coconut oil
- ¼ cup finely ground espresso or coffee beans
- 5 drops of essential oils of choice (rose, lavender, tea tree)

Application:

1. If you have whole beans, finely grind beans in a grinder. Beans should be finely ground so they do not scratch your skin.

2. Mix the Epsom salts, coffee and coconut oil in a bowl with a spoon. Add any essential oils.

3. Step into a bathtub. Put on loofah mitts or exfoliating gloves. If you do not have a bath mitt, don't worry; you can use your hands.

4. Take a spoonful of the mixture into your palms or your gloves and then rub the mixture all over your body in a circular motion. For tougher areas such as the knees, soles and elbows, spend extra scrubbing time. On places like the chest, neck, and stomach, where the skin is thinner, take it easy with the scrubbing and instead use cleanser on a washcloth to exfoliate. If you feel the salt or coffee is too harsh on your skin, rinse off the bath mitts and then spoon only the oil onto the mitts to continue.

5. Once your entire body is scrubbed well, rinse thoroughly.

6. Pat your skin dry. The salt will have exfoliated your skin nicely with the help of the loofah and the oil should leave skin soft and moisturized. You shouldn't even need to follow the bath with a moisturizer, but it never hurts to add more moisturizer.

*WARNING – the oil in this scrub can build up on your bathtub. Make sure to clean this after your scrub so the next person who gets in your bath doe not slip.

Day 18: Epsom Salt Bath with Essential Oils

Ingredients:

- 3-4 cups Epsom salts
- 5-10 drops of essential oils (optional)

Application:

1. Fill the bathtub with hot or warm water. Add about three to four cups of Epsom salts to the water. Swirl the water with your hands and allow the Epsom salts to dissolve.

2. Enhance your Epsom salt bath with five to ten drops of your favorite essential oils. Add lavender, rose or chamomile essential oil to relieve stress. Add the essential oils just before you step into the tub, as essential oils evaporate quickly in warm water.

3. Relax and soak in the Epsom salt bath for ten to fifteen minutes.

4. Take a warm shower to rinse the Epsom salts from your skin.

5. Apply moisturizer.

Day 19: Thai Massage / Thai Stretch

The benefits of massage demonstrate that it is an effective treatment for reducing stress, pain and muscle tension.

Beyond the benefits for specific conditions or diseases, some people enjoy massage because it often involves caring, comfort, and a sense of relaxation.

Inquire in your local area of a respected, certified and *gentle* Thai massage therapist. If you have any injuries, it may not be advisable to get a Thai massage. Please consult with your doctor. A Gentle Stretch session or a Swedish massage can be scheduled in the place of a Thai massage.

Day 20: Coffee & Egg Facial

Ingredients:

- 4 tbsp finely ground espresso or coffee beans
- 1 raw egg
- 2 tbsp honey

Application:

1. If you have whole beans, finely grind beans in a grinder. Beans should be finely ground so they do not scratch your face.

2. Mix coffee and egg in a bowl. Stir until a smooth paste forms. You can add more coffee if you like a thicker paste.

3. Stir in the honey (warm honey mixes better)

4. Apply the paste to your clean face and neck.

5. Allow the mask to dry.

6. Wet a washcloth and press it to your face to loosen the mask, follow by rinsing with warm water.

7. Follow with a thin layer of moisturizer.

Day 21: Haircut and/or Professional Blow dry

A new haircut means new life for your hair, and having a great haircut simply feels great. Trimming split ends from your hair regularly ensures it continues to grow well and stays healthy at all times. In addition, maintaining your hair also helps it grow faster and can improve its appearance greatly.

Inquire in your local area of a respected and certified hair stylist, or look around for someone with a cut you like and ask them where they go.

If you are not due for a haircut, schedule a blow dry for the hands-on attention and professional style. Enjoy looking and feeling confident.

Chapter 7: Conclusion

As you transition back to your work, relationships, hobbies and meals, maintain the mindfulness and self-realizations that you cultivated during The Dharma Zone. Eat with consciousness, listen attentively, love with sincerity, move joyfully, play with gratitude, live truthfully, and most importantly, be you.

From The Author

I wrote this book after a very difficult period in my life. In 2009, I found myself in a mentally, emotionally and physically abusive relationship. Having had a very distinct contrast from the healthy, joyful life I lived beforehand, I refused to accept the state of my mind and spirit after that relationship. I searched to discover why and how my mind could be altered without my permission. I worked to find a way to re-gain control of my mind, as I already understood this was the source reason that my life was not as bright and fluid as it had always been. My energies were blocked and my health was suffering as a result.

As I Am is a collection of the wisdom and practices that helped me to heal and regain control of my life. My journey back to me is how The Dharma Zone was created. My hope is that this program also helps you to become one with yourself, and to grow stronger in that truth every day.

"The more you know yourself, the more clarity there is. Self-knowledge has no end – you don't come to an achievement, you don't come to a conclusion. It is an endless river." ~ *Unknown*

Made in the USA
San Bernardino, CA
24 March 2013